SKI *with us*

BY PROFESSOR FRANZ HOPPICHLER

THE TEACHING METHOD OF THE AUSTRIAN SKI SCHOOL

in association with

PELHAM BOOKS

We should like to express our sincere thanks to Professor Robert Mader of the Austrian Ministry of Education, Art and Sport; to Professor Franz Hoppichler for all his kind help, invaluable advice and technical contribution in the preparation of this book; to the Austrian Ski Demo Team who, under Professor Hoppichler's direction, so brilliantly demonstrated the instructional sequences; and to all the staff at the Bundessportheim for their kind help.

A special thanks is due to President Erich Blachfelder of the Austrian Professional Ski Instructors' Association and his staff, to Mr Toni Sailer for the chapter on children's skiing and Mr Karl Schranz for the chapter on ski schools.

We are also most grateful, for all their assistance to Mr Erich Hotter and his staff at the Austrian National Tourist Office, London; Mr Wagner and his staff at the St Anton Tourist Office; Mr Schwartzler at Lech Tourist Office; Dr Ziepl and his staff at Kitzbühel Tourist Office; and Mr Wörgötter at Kitzbühel Museum.

Finally, a very special word of appreciation and thanks to Kjell Langset, the photographer, who so vividly captured the ski instructional sequences and set a new standard in ski photography.

James Wotton and Graham Davis.

Ski With Us was conceived, edited and designed by James Wotton Limited, 7 Stafford Mansions, Albert Bridge Road, London SW11, and Graham Davis Associates, 10 Amwell Street, London EC1.

First published in Great Britain by

Pelham Books Ltd.
44 Bedford Square
London WC1B 3DP
1985

Hoppichler, Franz
Ski With Us; the teaching method of the Austrian Ski School.
1. Skis and Skiing
1. Title   II Ski mit uns *English*.

796.93 GV 854

ISBN 0 7207 1638 1
Photography by Kjell Langset
Typeset by IC Dawkins Ltd.
Colour separations by Excel Ltd.
Printed and bound in the Netherlands by Royal Smeets Offset, BV Weert.

CONTENTS

THE AUSTRIAN SKI SCHOOL

Austria has a long tradition of skiing and ski instruction which has influenced the lives of many millions of people around the world. In a land in which tourism means so much, and where more than 10,000 ski instructors are employed in 400 ski schools, this is perhaps not surprising. Every day our ski instructors are ready to help you – not only to improve your skiing technique and make it more versatile, but also to ensure that your holiday is as enjoyable as possible.

An important aspect of the Austrian Ski School is its adaptability. It took a commanding role in the development of skiing, and it has met the demands placed upon it by the international tourist industry in an impressive manner. Austrian ski schools now cater for more than a million people every year.

In the 1960s Austrian experts turned their attention to ski instruction for children and developed suitable teaching methods. 'Play and learn' was their motto. The 'ski kindergarten' has since sprung up everywhere in Austrian ski schools, making ski instruction for the whole family a reality at last. The Austrian Ski School and Austrian manufacturers work closely to ensure that the best equipment is available for learner and racer alike.

The Austrian Ski School did much to promote cross-country skiing and ski touring. Then deep powder skiing triggered off a tidal wave of interest, and with it came extensions to the existing programme of safety education.

Helicopter skiing is the newest innovation — and an exciting one too. Those who are sufficiently capable are flown by helicopter high onto our mountains where they can experience — not totally without restraint, but with enormous pleasure — the exhilaration of deep snow. This type of skiing has brought a whole new dimension to the sport.

In Austria's ski schools racing gets a fair deal too. Every ski school holds speed trials and many also stage the WISBI races in order to compare their pupils' performances with those of the world's top skiers.

The achievements of Austria's ski schools are only possible because each teacher has behind him a total of 30 weeks' intensive training. Yet even experienced teachers cannot rest on their laurels and the regular refresher courses they are obliged to take guarantee that you will be taught according to

the most modern methods and be given much useful advice on matters in general.

As teachers, guides and helpful companions our motto is 'Always at your service!' We want to help you enjoy your skiing holiday to the full and really improve your technique. This book shows you how. Have a great time!

Erich Blachfelder
President of the Austrian Professional
Ski Instructors' Association

7

THE HISTORY OF AUSTRIAN SKIING

The industrialization that occurred in the late 19th century made factory work increasingly monotonous and exhausting. Little wonder, then, that people ventured out into the wide open spaces for both relaxation and sport. The expedition by Fridtjof Nansen across the southern tip of Greenland in 1888 gave particular momentum to this trend. His book *Across Greenland on Snowshoes* was published in 1891. In it he described skis and skiing in great detail and effectively started the first boom in skiing. The sport took off in many countries.

Some of the earliest skiing in Austria took place in the Krainer mountains in the Pacher range. In 1887 Viktor Sohm from Bregenz carried out his first experiments and the Styrians Max Kleinoschegg and Toni Schruf, like all Austrians at that time, tried out Norwegian skis but later constructed their own skis better suited to alpine terrain. As early as 1893 Franz Reisch climbed the Kitzbühler Horn and also founded the WSV (winter sports club) in Kitzbühel. A year later the skiing section of the Alpine Club in Innsbruck was formed and in 1901 the Arlberg Ski Club was founded.

ZDARSKY THE FOUNDING FATHER

Born in Inglau (Mähren) in 1856, Matthias Zdarsky lost an eye early in life and in 1889 retreated to the Habernreit estate near Lilienfeld. In these mountainous surroundings he worked on the technology of skis and bindings. As a result of his refinements the Norwegian ski, originally 2.4m long, became shorter and the groove in the running surface disappeared. After many experiments a way was found to make the binding laterally rigid yet allow forward release. The 'running ski' thus became a 'turning ski'. The long 'Zdarsky lance' was used as a pole for balancing and as an aid to turning.

In 1896 Zdarsky's book *Alpine (Lilienfeld) Ski Technique* appeared. As a contrast to the skiing technique of the Norwegians which required great skill and balance, Zdarsky's aim was a technique which would enable anybody to learn to ski quickly and safely on difficult terrain. His method was based on slow and safe skiing in the stem position, and he instructed vast numbers of pupils in alpine skills.

Serious disagreements soon arose with the representatives of the Scandinavian, and more especially Norwegian, ski school—a dispute which was fought on a very personal level. To put an end to this argument over technique, a giant slalom race was held on the Muckenkogel in 1905. The vertical height, gradient and length of the race were specified precisely and agreed, and the course was very clearly marked out. When Zdarsky won by a convincing margin the dispute died away.

In 1900 Zdarsky had founded the International Alpine Ski Club in Vienna, and for his efforts in adapting both the equipment and the technique to the steep slopes of the Alps, he was rightly acknowledged by Sir Arnold Lunn as the 'Father of Alpine Skiing'. From that point on skiing really became alpine.

War brings changes to most things and skiing was no exception. Even Zdarsky was an instructor in the Austrian army, where he indirectly influenced Colonel Bilgeri, and it was a pupil of both Bilgeri and Zdarsky, Major Theodor von Lerch, who introduced skiing to Japan in 1910. Bilgeri himself

FATHER OF ALPINE SKIING

Matthias Zdarsky (opposite) thought logically and was clever with his hands. He adapted Norwegian skiing equipment to alpine terrain (top) with a binding which could release forwards but not sideways, a shorter ski which was easier to turn, and a long 'lance'. Above all, he made stemming the basis of fast and safe learning. His innovations enabled skiing to become an alpine sport

SKI JUMPING

At the first Tyrolean Ski Championships in 1905 Josef Wallner won the 20 m jump

FORMATIVE INFLUENCES

Fridtjof Nansen's crossing of southern Greenland on skis in 1888 prompted many to try skiing for themselves. When war broke out in Europe it was essential for soldiers to be mobile in winter. Colonel Bilgeri adopted some of Zdarsky's methods but also Norwegian elements. He taught soldiers the stem turn for safe descent (from Zdarsky) and the use of two sticks for walking and climbing (like the Norwegians)

SCHNEIDER'S WORLD ROLE

A naturally talented skier who grew up in the Stuben area, Hannes Schneider was influenced by Bilgeri. The stem Christiania and also the sheared Christiania skied in short swings were the basis of his teaching. Superb photographs,

informative stop-action multiple shots and, in particular, pioneering films by Dr Arnold Franck and racing victories by Schneider all advanced the teaching and the spread of skiing. Firmly established as an influential ski instructor in Austria, Schneider became a guiding light abroad as well

was concerned with the military aspects of skiing. His book *Alpine Skiing* (1910) enjoyed a wide readership.

Bilgeri's technique was close to that of Zdarsky, but he used skis with a groove and a pair of sticks instead of one. The two-stick method was necessary because the army needed good balance to carry heavy packs. In 1898 Bilgeri led an eight-man expedition on the first ski tour of the Tuxer mountains and by 1905 the Austrian army was organizing its own instruction. Due to Bilgeri's initiative, over 6000 skis a year were produced from 1906 and these were available to the police force, the post office and the forestry commission as well as the general public. During the First World War companies of mountain guides were formed and the ski service of the Austro-Hungarian army was organized.

In the 1920s Bilgeri often travelled abroad to help form alpine companies in other armies. As many young skiers had been trained in Bilgeri's methods during the First World War, the post-war era saw a sudden rise in the number of similarly trained qualified ski instructors.

Born in 1890 in Stuben by the Arlberg, Hannes Schneider

attracted attention through his early success in skiing and as a result of this he was brought to St Anton as a ski instructor by the hotelier Schuler. In the First World War he was taught by Bilgeri and saw service on the South Tyrolean front.

In 1920 he resumed his career as a ski instructor and in 1922 founded the Arlberg Ski School where his 'Arlberg technique' was taught in week-long courses. Characteristic features of the technique were schussing in the Arlberg crouch, the wide-track stance, stem turns for ski touring, stem christies and pulled christies for closely linked turns.

Back in 1912 Dr Arnold Franck had been in the process of writing a book on skiing when he saw Schneider and the Swiss Capiti in action. The book was not finished until after the war, but *Wunder des Schneeschuhs* (Miracle of the Snow Shoe) had an enormous impact throughout the world. The time-lapse photographs were a sensation at that time, for they provided information not previously available. Several films on the theme followed production of the book, enticing people into the cinemas and then onto the snow. Slow motion photography, action camera work, telephoto shots,

DIFFERENCES OF VIEW

Earlier this century, long skis, low speeds and deep snow meant that the skis had to be turned with the body, but racing experience convinced Toni Ducia and Kurt Reinl that good control, not turning, was the most important aspect of skiing – and that good control meant *not* rotating the body with the skis. By contrast Dr Fritz Hoschek held that the most effective way to turn was to rotate the entire body. This, however, resulted in many accidents

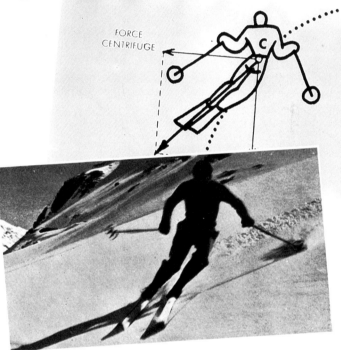

FORCE CENTRIFUGE

frontlighting, enthusiastic crowd scenes and informative glimpses of experts at work inspired many thousands to acquire the necessary skills for skiing.

Hannes Schneider gave a new impetus to skiing, even in Japan, which caused it to eventually become a sport for the masses. He sowed a seed from which millions of people around the world would eventually reap the benefits.

Schneider also provided the momentum for skiing in the United States, having emigrated there before the Second World War. By virtue of his personality and expertise he contributed significantly to the post-war upsurge in winter sports, instruction and racing in America.

Although it gained little recognition at first, the invention by Rudolf Lettner from Hallein of the steel edge, in 1930, gave skiing another forward push, enabling faster and safer skiing and tighter turns. For a seemingly 'minor' innovation, the consequences that flowed from it were considerable.

Although Hannes Schneider did teach skiers to turn their body, as a racer he also sensed that only a less twisted torso could steer the skis well and with subtlety. This point was

taken up by Toni Ducia and Kurt Reinl, trainers and racers for the Ski Club of Paris in the 1930s. As racing skiers they stressed the importance of the untwisted position of the body to and from the fall-line; good control was their main concern. They felt that the powerful forces arising beyond the fall-line could only be compensated for if the body was held in an untwisted position above the skis and ready to move. They were thus early proponents of the 'basic position' so important today.

At a time when skiing lessons meant slow skiing, when there were no prepared pistes and the skis were relatively long, the emphasis was on turning. As a result the call by Ducia and Reinl for good control went largely unheard.

Dr Fritz Hoschek devoted himself to the problem of turning the skis. He recognized that the entire body had to be rotated with great strength in order to turn the long skis against the high resistance encountered at low speeds. This, however, subjected the knees and ankles in particular to undue stress, resulting in fractures and many accidents. The solution to the problem came with advances in technique and technology.

Skiing quickly became a racing sport and international competitions were held. One of the most important Austrian racing skiers of the 1930s whose contribution cannot be overlooked was Toni Seelos from Seefeld who emulated the elegance and success of his hero Benno Leubner. His aim was to link his turns together as tightly as possible and in order to achieve this he began to unweight and turn both skis simultaneously.

The 'Father of the Parallel Turn', as he became known, succeeded in his objective. In slalom races his lead over his opponents was sometimes as much as 9 seconds.

Parallel skiing became the new fashion, and a lasting one too, especially in teaching circles. Whole doctrines of skiing were based on it and these included the 'méthode française' adopted by Emile Allais, a future world champion.

After the Second World War skiing in Austria slowly came to life again and instruction continued to show traces of two different approaches. The Arlberg school, following Zdarsky's emphasis on safety, taught an exaggerated stem position that restricted the skier's freedom and flow of movement. On the other hand there were the ideas of Hoschek, Seelos and Allais, advocates of parallel skiing and rotation of the whole body — a straightforward basis for learning, but one that was difficult for beginners. Both schools thus had advantages and drawbacks.

FOCUS ON THE LEGS

The divisions remained for a long time. Gradually, however, young racers started to perform movements belonging to neither school. They too turned, but only with their legs and therefore more quickly. They rotated the torso in the opposite direction to the legs — the 'reverse shoulder technique'. Increasing attention was paid to the legs. 'Leg play' was gaining ground. More fun, more dance-like, and because of the closed skis, more elegant, this style became the fashion.

It was a development that would have been slower (or might not have taken place at all) without Professor Stefan Kruckenhauser. He believed that it is the legs and not the body which should turn the skis; the body should be used to compensate for this and maintain overall balance. Ridiculed and disputed at first, his views were finally accepted.

Starting in 1955 the 'wedeln' (literally tail-wagging) went round the world and millions enjoyed the fun of the new technique. The 'swinging' turns became not only faster but also more precise. Above all, deep powder snow was no longer forbidden territory, but a playground for those who wanted to move in this rhythmic way. Skiers were fascinated by the new style.

Turning on, and later in, the snow became easier at first with the short ski and subsequently with the flexible metal and plastic ski. The consequences were smooth round turns and deep snow skiing, even for children.

THE RACING TRADITION

Organized ski racing had been initiated by Sir Arnold Lunn, who was born in 1888. He took sporting Englishmen to the races held at Mürren in Switzerland for which General Roberts of Kandahar had donated a victory cup and created the Roberts of Kandahar Challenge. Together with Hannes Schneider in 1928 Lunn created the Arlberg-Kandahar race and can thus be regarded as the 'Father of Alpine Racing'. The disciplines of

FATHER OF THE PARALLEL TURN

Toni Seelos (below) sought to turn the skis simultaneously and as quickly as possible. Initially attracting attention because of his elegance and then through slalom victories, he came to dominate the Austrian racing scene and be called the 'Father of the Parallel Turn'. His influence as a trainer was even greater. Many teams, in particular the French, benefited from his help

downhill, slalom and the alpine combination were officially recognized by the FIS in 1930.

Rudi Matt carried on the traditions of the Kandahar, which was not easy, since commercial and other powerful new influences began to tarnish the lustre of the event. Yet he managed to establish himself, being receptive to good new ideas and sceptical of change for change's sake.

National squads were set up and victories soon were celebrated. New talent emerged from the Kitzbühel ski club. Competition and challenge created the 'wonder team' of Sailer, Molterer, Pravda, Hinterseer, Leitner and Huber who carried the glory of Austria around the world. Glory was followed by exports: skis, clothing, bindings, technology and lifts, all made in Austria.

Karl Schranz from Arlberg, whose unconventional approach often made him a lonely figure, brightened up the Austrian racing scene with scintillating victories, strong views and a modern approach in keeping with the changing, more business-like world of skiing. As he has shown, sacrifice is often necessary to bring about the changes required for the beneficial development of the sport overall.

IMPORTANT INNOVATORS

The Kandahar race is closely linked with the names of Sir Arnold Lunn (below right) and Rudi Matt (left). Both fought for the Alpine combination and defended it as far as the World Cup. Skiing soon became a sport for millions. In racing the 'dream team' (above) took the world by storm and subsequently Karl Schranz (right) took a new technique – the wedeln – around the world. Wedeln was started on its journey by Professor Kruckenhauser (circular picture). His ideas on wedeln and the 'leg action' technique revolutionized the sport

ST CHRISTOPH

The Federal Ski School at St
Christoph gave momentum to
skiing from as early as 1922
when students were taught by
Professor Janner. In 1924 the
school was taken over by the
Federal Ministry for Education
and since 1927 it has been the
centre for ski teachers'
examinations. The school was
adapted to modern course
teaching methods by Professor
Kruckenhauser with several
extensions to the building. The
success of the wedeln made St
Christoph the centre of
development of technique and
methodology. The Federal Ski
School is the red building in the
photograph

FEDERAL SKI SCHOOLS

The Austrian government is bound by law to promote sport and in skiing it is particularly active. Although the teaching of skiing and the training and testing of instructors is governed by the individual federal states, the central government has, in agreement with the states, been responsible for the education and examination of federal ski teachers since 1927. The idea is sponsorship without interference, allowing federal and state government to cooperate in the development of skiing.

Since the 1920s the federal government has set up well-equipped centres, the Federal Ski Schools, which are involved in all aspects of skiing. There are now schools at St Christoph, Obergurgl, Kitzsteinhorn, Hintermoos and Obertaun. St Christoph is the centre where most instructors are trained.

St Christoph has been extended over the years to meet changing requirements and can now accommodate 164 people on courses of up to five weeks. It has a 200-seat lecture theatre, two seminar rooms, a day room, dining hall, table tennis room, small hall, weight-training room, modern ski and boot storage areas and generously equipped sports halls, all purpose-built. Highly experienced teachers are on hand to give lessons on a wide range of topics and it is these instructors who form the Ski Demo Team which represents Austria at 'Interski' congresses. It is these same teachers who demonstrate the ski techniques in this book.

The courses focus on the training of ski teachers and the ski-training of sports teachers, the Austrian army and police.

Courses are based on the most up-to-date information, and research projects and practical experiments form an important part of the school's work. Most programmes of ski instruction must be approved by St Christoph. In particular, however, the correct techniques and methods for teaching different categories of pupil (whether children or adults) is carefully specified. Other regulations govern such things as length of instruction and the degree of difficulty for different categories of training.

The influence of the teaching at St Christoph has spread around the world. Pupils and experts from many countries visit the school to take part in courses and exchange ideas. Wherever you ski you are likely to find 'Christophers' reminiscing about the time they spent at the school. Teachers

BENEFITS OF RESEARCH

Research is being carried out into many aspects of skiing, including the stresses exerted upon the body during different types of turn. As a result of such study, for example, skis on average are weighted 25 per cent more at the tails; it has been found that the outside ski edge is best unweighted; up-unweighting affects balance more than is commonly thought; ice is more of a hindrance to turning than gradient; and up to 280 per cent of body weight can be exerted on the outer ski during a turn

also visit other countries as ambassadors of skiing.

The Federal Ministry of Education, Art and Sport in Austria arranges courses to introduce skiing to those who often have to concern themselves with the sport in a professional capacity — people such as sports equipment dealers, doctors specializing in sports injuries, judges, diplomats, foresters and the like.

TRAINING AN INSTRUCTOR

It takes a long time to become an Austrian ski teacher. The process starts with two to three years of practical experience gained in local ski schools. Guided by experienced teachers, the trainee gradually grows in proficiency until he receives the qualifications required for teaching beginners.

After a probationary period he attends two three-week training courses to provincial standard, after which a stiff exam has to be sat and which always eliminates a large number of applicants. Apart from the details of skiing technique and teaching methods, these courses teach the young candidates how a ski teacher should behave on the open slopes, where he carries full responsibility, to keep himself and his pupils out of danger.

Having passed the provincial teacher's exam, it's back to the practical work. After two or three years the head of the ski school submits the candidate for the entrance examination for training to federal standard. This training is extremely rigorous. If he scores just one bad mark in a slalom, or say in free skiing with a class, the candidate has to start the course again the following year. Out of 200 applicants only between 50 and 70 are usually accepted.

The prospective ski teacher then completes two theoretical courses and two practical courses of four and a half weeks and three weeks each respectively. Whoever wishes can, after a preparatory course, take the ski guide course which prepares the candidate especially for off-piste skiing, but is also an opening to training as a mountain guide. But again and again between the courses there is more practice, which is observed, guided and finally assessed by the head of the ski school.

Your ski instructor is thus trained to the highest standards and you can put your trust in him with confidence. His skill in technique, method and safety is self-evident, while his qualities as both leader and companion will soon become obvious to you.

THE ST CHRISTOPH SCHOOL

Since the 1920s the Federal Ski School at St Christoph has devised many new methods and techniques and conducts a continuous programme of research and experiment. It is the place where most instructors' courses end and further training takes place

GETTING FIT

Skiing involves both physical manipulation and travel at speed, and also coping with forces which exert pressures on the legs averaging 200 kg and sometimes reaching 300 kg. On icy surfaces the weight is continually switched from ski to ski, which demands strength, again especially in the legs.

Consequently, if your legs are not strong enough they will tense up as your speed, and thus the pressure, increases. And if your legs are tense you will make one mistake after another.

When your skis are gliding or skidding you need strength in movement. In order to be able to react to all the shocks to your sense of balance, you need dynamic strength.

INDOOR PREPARATION

To prepare yourself for skiing, keep a close watch on everyday movements in the weeks beforehand. Keep your knees straight when you bend the hips. Lift something off the floor, keeping arms and legs straight. Think about every movement you make. Don't miss an opportunity to balance on one leg on a narrow surface, and when you have to fetch something, take longer strides and as you do so, go into a low straddle position to stretch your leg muscles even more.

INDOOR EXERCISES

The muscles at the front of the legs and in the abdomen are used in skiing to bring the body from the backward lean to the forward lean position as is necessary when we are accelerated down the fall-line.

To get these muscles toned up here are some simple exercises you can do in your own home.

- In a standing position, raise your toes until you can feel the strain in your shin muscles.
- Lie on your back, then sit up sharply, keeping your legs straight and your heels on the ground. Vary this exercise by rotating the shoulders to the left or right as you sit up.
- Try to do 10 sit ups to start with and gradually increase the numbers and speed with which you do them.
- Stepping up on to a bench (for example) develops the muscles in the legs most used in skiing.
- The balance platform (shown opposite) is a simple but very effective way to improve your balance.

In conjunction with the individual exercises, try to make all the movements you would on skis, from the snow plough to the eight key swings (see pages 46/49). Of course, your body will not move in exactly the same way, but as you make the actions form a mental picture and imagine you're on the ski slopes. Then speed up your work rate. You'll find it stimulating and your limbs will start to be prepared for the real thing.

Practice your rhythm too, try some wedeln steps (page 68/69), in quick succession, and again create a mental image of these actions on the slopes.

OUTDOOR EXERCISE

As the autumn leaves begin to fall, why not slip on your tracksuit and get out and about? Go for a brisk walk, varying the pace and the length of your strides. Pay attention to your breathing and try consciously to breathe in time with your steps.

Concentrate not just on exercise but also on recovery. Check your pulse; if it does not return to normal quickly enough, exercise for shorter periods and less energetically. Alternate between exercise and recovery, and while recovering do a few loosening and stretching exercises.

It does not matter which exercises you do to prepare yourself for skiing, but it is important that you make a conscious effort. Take cross-country runs, up and down hills. It will help you to adapt your pace to uneven ground and help you to react quickly to keep your balance.

If you live near a hilly area, augment this build up with some fell walking or moorland treks. Take your ski poles with you, and use them to help you up the hills and to slow you down on the descents. This will develop your arm and leg muscles and your general co-ordination. It will also teach you to be adaptable, and adaptability is what skiing is all about.

GRADUAL BUILD-UP

Exercise with a partner or even your whole family, but always in brief sessions to avoid the risk of cramp. It is better to do a few exercises several times a day than a lot at once. Jump from side to side, first on both feet, then hopping on one foot. The more you bend your knees now, the less often you will be brought down on your knees when skiing.

Gradually increase the amount of exercise, always starting with the simplest ones to warm up the muscles. Don't forget to exercise the upper body as well. Stretch a scarf or towel above your head and swing your arms back as far as possible and from side to side. If you can feel the strain in your muscles, you know you are on the way to making your body more supple.

ALL TOGETHER

If you would like to, exercise with friends or even join a club. In a group of people with similar interests the team spirit will keep you going, even if you sometimes do not feel like it; those that join reluctantly often have an enjoyable time. In a group you can also exercise with a partner, pushing against his weight to stretch and loosen up your muscles. You can learn from a partner, too, watching him repeat exactly what you do.

If you like dancing you can combine this with training and perhaps join an aerobics or dance group. One advantage of exercising to music is that it keeps you going when you think you have run out of steam and the perspiration is beginning to flow. Another advantage is the sense of rhythm it encourages, which is also important in skiing. Here too, a partner helps to make the exercise more enjoyable. The important thing is to exercise regularly every day, starting slowly and gently, then gradually increasing the duration and intensity of the exercises.

So there are many ways in which you can prepare yourself well for skiing. Keep fit through the summer by playing tennis or golf, or by swimming or cycling. Walking and climbing are particularly good forms of exercise for keeping you in touch with the kind of terrain on which you will be executing your turns in the winter.

The leg muscles are, of course, very important for skiing, but so are the abdominal muscles. Keeping your feet held still, raise and lower your upper body; or keep your body still and raise and lower your legs, with twisting movements as well. Finally, raise both arms and legs into the 'jack-knife' position, which will be useful later when 'carving'

The legs have to bend and stretch continually when you are skiing, so practise this exercise often – high and low, fast and slow, just like the real thing

Step-ups give you the strength needed to work against your weight and later against the force generated by the swing (turn). A lack of strength results in tenseness, which causes mistakes. Work up a sweat – it's good for the circulation!

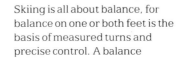

Skiing is all about balance, for balance on one or both feet is the basis of measured turns and precise control. A balance platform like the one shown here is a useful aid to help your training. It's the sort of thing you can use in your own home

EQUIPMENT: CHOICE OF CLOTHES

Because skiing is a technical sport it is important that the equipment you choose is not only appropriate but also of good quality. Don't buy without thinking. Try and get some advice from experienced skiers. With the right equipment you are half-way to success in skiing.

For a sport that is practised outdoors in the coldest season of the year it is essential to have the correct clothing. You should feel happy with what you wear and it can be as colourful and fashionable as you like, but it must also serve a purpose, so don't buy because of fashion alone.

When choosing ski wear in a sports shop, try it on first but don't just stand in front of the mirror; bend and stretch and swing your arms and legs. If the clothes do not restrict your movement, they will be suitable.

NEXT TO THE SKIN

Let's start closest to the skin. Modern ski underwear is made of materials which 'breathe' and absorb perspiration and is tailored so that movement is not restricted. When buying underwear, however, remember that you will not only be skiing but will also be sitting down to 5 o'clock tea. What may be very functional on the slopes may be unsuitable for lunch time and for après ski. Remember too that you may experience very cold weather but also warm weather during your holiday, and that you will need spare clothing.

There are basically two types of ski clothing. Firstly, the ski pullover, ski pants and light anorak. Then, for colder weather, quilted salopettes or overalls are essential. Modern materials for anoraks and overalls are expensive, but they guarantee that the clothes will 'breathe' while keeping out the damp.

If you feel the cold a lot, buy mittens instead of gloves. Gloves are the obvious choice for the sporting skier and for warmer spring weather.

You need your head for more than skiing, so protect it well! Choose a warm hat which will cover your ears when required. An indispensable piece of equipment is a pair of goggles, but don't skimp on quality, since cheap goggles can lead to snow blindness and inflammation of the eyes.

SWEATERS FOR WARMTH

It is a good idea to take at least a couple of sweaters with you, for they will have a dual role to play: first and foremost they will keep you warm, and they should also look good for après ski. Make sure that they are sufficiently long in the body and arms so that your skin or under garments are not exposed to the elements no matter how energetic you are. If your neck and wrists are exposed you will feel the cold very quickly, so a roll-neck sweater or a zip-up polyester/cotton shirt is worth considering. A scarf will come in useful, and can look stylish.

Your skin will take a pounding from the sun's rays, icy winds, and contact with the snow. It is very important that you use a facial sun cream or lotion on your face and a lip salve for your lips. Moisturising cream will help prevent your skin from drying out.

DRESSED FOR THE SLOPES

You may prefer a one-piece suit or a combination of ski pants and pullover/anorak. Gloves are for racers and warmer days; mittens keep out the cold best. And don't forget a woolly hat! Pick quality goggles with anti-mist vents, and always take spare clothing

By placing the gloved hand through the handle's strap you have a better chance of keeping hold of the stick should you fall

EQUIPMENT: SKIS

All skiers know that they require, apart from suitable clothing,

- skis
- ski boots
- safety bindings with ski stoppers or straps
- ski sticks

It is, however, easy to overlook important points when considering the purchase of individual items. The right choice not only contributes to your enjoyment of skiing but is also an important factor affecting your safety on the piste. Where safety is concerned only those items of equipment which conform to international standards should be used.

Ski manufacturers produce skis to suit all abilities and an ambitious beginner need no longer be put off skiing by having to slog around on skis too long for him.

Skis are divided into four main groups:

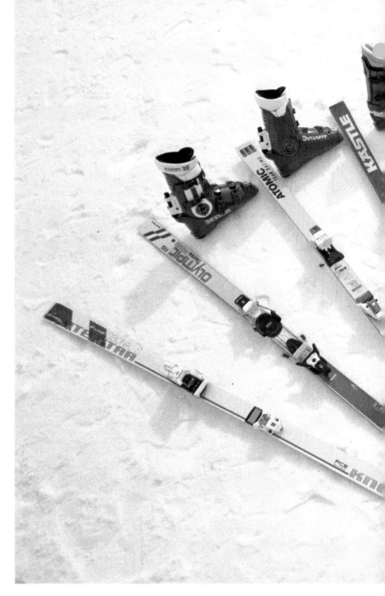

GROUP	TYPE OF SKI	CHARACTERISTICS	RECOMMENDED LENGTH
S	Sports	Tracks very well, but only turns well if precisely controlled	Women: height + 15 to 20 cm Men: height + 20 to 30 cm
A	Allround, compact, mid	Turns easily and tracks well	Women and men: height + 5 to 15 cm
L	Short	Turns very easily but does not track well	Women and men: height − 10 to + 5 cm
I		This group covers all skiers with individual requirements who cannot be assigned to groups S, A and L (e.g. freestyle skiers, slalom racers).	

For children and teenagers the following guidelines apply on ski length:

	up to 10 years	10-14 years	14-16 years
Beginners	chin height	eye height	body height
Intermediate	nose height	body height	height + 5 cm
Advanced	body height	height + 5 cm	height + 10 cm
Sports	height + 5 cm	height + 10 cm	height + 20 cm

For both children and adults the range of recommended sizes within each group depends on ability (shorter skis turn more easily, longer skis give better tracking).

When buying skis you should note the following points:

- Skis which conform to International standards have a line or arrow to show where the centre of the boot should be when locked in the binding
- You can insure skis against theft or breakage when you buy them. Always get the policy stamped by the dealer

MAINTENANCE CHECKLIST

Correct ski maintenance will mean that your skis will keep their value longer and retain their characteristics:

- Repair running surface damage with plastic 'candle' or repair chips
- Sand or file edges regularly with a small hand-file
- Larger repairs should be carried out by the manufacturer, but first take your damaged skis to a reputable sports shop
- Always use a ski bag for transporting skis on a car roofrack, otherwise salt spray from the road will corrode edges and bindings
- The right ski wax helps the ski to glide and turn more effectively

There is nothing wrong in looking for a bargain, but to buy poor quality equipment or failing to replace old equipment that has clearly had its day is simply to tempt fate and invite the risk of injury.

CHOICE OF SKIS

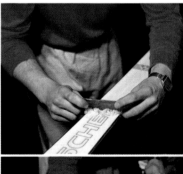

Most skis are well made but they must be chosen to suit your size, weight, speed and ability. Seek assistance from knowledgeable shop staff. It is essential to choose skis appropriate for your level of skill. Have the bindings fitted at the shop. If you can't decide at once, hire some skis to try them out, but make sure they are well-maintained otherwise the comparison is pointless. Consider whether good edging or easy and comfortable turning is more important to you. The shorter the ski the easier it is to turn, but if it is too short it loses stability. Have your skis serviced regularly. This will aid your technical improvement

SKI PREPARATION

Clean the running surface and remove wax with a scraper, then make it smooth. File the edges, first underneath and then the sides. Wax the skis using dry, tube or hot wax and scrape off the excess. Best of all, have your skis prepared at a sports shop that performs this service

CARRYING SKIS

Fix your skis together with the ski stoppers. Carry them on your shoulder with the points forward and your sticks in the other hand. Take care not to decapitate anyone by turning round quickly! Put your skis on before queuing for a lift, or carry them upright before joining a cable car queue

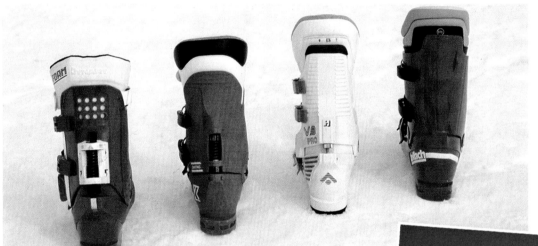

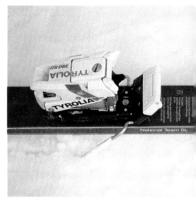

First and foremost ski boots should fit well and be comfortable. They need to be a snug fit in order to transmit leg movements positively to the skis. When trying boots on wear only one pair of ski socks. Specify in the shop whether you require recreational, allround or racing boots. For convenience choose a rear-entry boot. Choose foam or similar material for the best fit, and check that you can open and close the clips on your own. Never stand your boots near sources of heat

EQUIPMENT: BOOTS AND BINDINGS

Ski boots should first and foremost be comfortable and allow the skis to be steered accurately. When buying,

● Wear only one pair of ski socks when trying boots on
● Walk around the shop in the boots for about *half an hour*. Only then will the inner boot be supple enough to fit snugly
● The boots should not feel too tight at any part of the foot
   Some boot manufacturers classify their products according to the groups; beginners, good skiers and sports skiers.
● Beginners (Recreational boot): a lower boot which does not force the wearer into the forward lean stance.
Suitable for beginners and intermediates; ideal for slow to average speeds
● Good skiers (Allround boot): a somewhat higher boot with inbuilt and to some degree adjustable forward lean. For intermediate to very good skiers. Ideal for medium to high speeds; guarantees good tracking and edging
● Sports skiers (Racing boot): guarantees precise tracking and edging even at high speeds
   Remember to always store your boots with the clips closed.

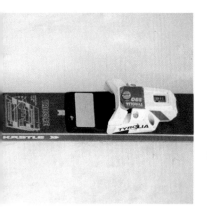

BEST BINDINGS

Bindings hold the boot onto the ski during skiing while having the ability to release it in the event of an emergency (below). Only buy bindings that have ski stoppers, and make sure that the bindings are fitted and adjusted by experts. Overhaul your bindings before use each season. Always clean all snow off the soles of boots before stepping into bindings, and check for release before skiing by kicking with the other foot. The photos show the boot being placed toe-first into the binding, the boot and binding locked together, and the ski pole being used to release the boot from the binding when the skier is stationary

THE SAFETY BINDING

The safety binding has to fulfil two functions: to bind the boot firmly to the ski, and to release the boot and thus prevent injury when the skier falls.

The release setting of the binding mechanism is determined by the diameter of the top of the shin bone (tibia). For the correct setting, the strength of this bone is the determining factor, not your body weight.

If properly maintained, ski bindings can outlast several pairs of skis. The following points are worth noting:

● Ski bindings should *only* be fitted and adjusted by experts. Manufacturers guarantee the correct functioning of their products only if they are correctly fitted and adjusted

● Ask your dealer for a certificate confirming the adjustment or release setting of your bindings

● Bindings should be overhauled and adjusted every year, and oiled or greased

● Corrosion can seriously affect the efficiency of bindings

Most modern bindings have integral ski stoppers, but retaining straps also have their advantages. The important thing is that all skis *must* be fitted with one of these two safety devices. The ski stopper reduces the risk of being hit by one of your own skis when you fall, and the retaining strap prevents the ski getting lost in deep snow.

FASHION
WITH WARMTH AND COMFORT

Skiing is more than a sport. It's exhilarating and exciting. To feel good you must feel warm and comfortable.

Not only must ski-wear be fashionable, it must also be specially designed for this dynamic sport.

Within the Sportsworld Department, C&A offers unbeatable value and a great selection of clothing and accessories for Men, Women and Children.

If you want the top range of ski-wear at C&A then look for the name Rodeo — the name for active sportswear.

RodeO

WARMING UP

Avoid arriving at the top of a lift stiff with cold – for a cold start is as bad for the human body as it is for an engine. So take the trouble to warm up before you ski off, just as racing skiers do.

The primary objective of warming up is, of course, to improve your performance, learn faster and move safely. A further aim, and just as important, is to gain greater enjoyment from every minute. You don't want to feel always as if you're 'on your last legs' and tensed up. Tense muscles are enemy number one in skiing. A third advantage of warming up is that you will enjoy long descents, you will ski 'andante' instead of 'staccato'. The stops become shorter and you will find that you can keep up with more experienced friends.

GENTLY DOES IT
Don't just warm up *before* you start, but take the first few turns gently as well, using easier types of turn which you are already good at. This will boost your self-confidence

and warm up and loosen the muscles on which you will later rely at higher speeds. For the first descent, forget the difficult piste which thrilled you yesterday – you will have to build up to that degree of skill again.

Above all, watch out for the peak performance periods during the day. These occur usually between 10.30 and 11 am and again around 2 pm. Make allowances in your speed and choice of piste for the periods around midday and 3 pm when performance generally wanes. The majority of accidents occur during these periods – and you don't want to be involved in one!

LOOSENING THE MUSCLES

Get warmed up! The muscles function better if they are loosened up first. The exercises shown on this page will help you achieve this. Start gently, avoiding any violent movements. One of the best ways to warm up is to start skiing slowly, making gentle turns, until you feel ready. Don't overstretch your muscles while you are still cold or you may end up pulling one

29

BASIC SKILLS: BALANCE, SCHUSS AND SNOWPLOUGH

Skiing is all about balancing, turning and control. In schussing (straight running), but more especially when turning, we balance by bending, straightening and turning our joints. We shift our weight forwards, backwards, right, left, up and down.

When you ski, the surface exerts accelerating and braking forces upon the skis. Acceleration forces cause your skis to shoot forward, leaving your upper body in the backward lean position. You therefore have to bend the ankle, knee and hip joints before you can straighten up again. Braking forces are caused either by the snow surface or when you turn your skis across the direction of travel. This results in your body being pushed into a forward lean. You can avoid this by leaning back before braking and letting the pressure bend your joints.

The moment you skid or turn, you are accelerated or slowed down in a sideways direction. If you ski in a wide-tracked stance your balance in this direction will be improved. When traversing a slope or moving in a long curve, the uphill or inner leg is bent more and you have to compensate in your balance.

If you skid sideways you'll have to swing your weight sideways too, but once you begin to ski faster you will ski more on the edges (carving) and will be able to shift the weight forwards and backwards along the whole length of the skis.

The arms are another important aid to balancing. If you are forced backwards, swing your arms forwards. If your skis suddenly accelerate, swing your arms backwards. If most of your weight is on the outer ski, the inner arm should be lifted

MAINTAINING BALANCE

The double exposure photograph at far left shows the correct balance on the skis at rest. The knees should be bent for the schuss. The skier at left, however, bends too much from the hips. Skiing is a matter of gliding and balancing. Your weight has to be shifted back and forth to compensate for accelerating and braking forces generated by the terrain or by turns. The basic work of balancing is achieved by tensing and relaxing the muscles

SCHUSSING

Schussing (straight running) is the first real test of balance. The skis must be steered, and braking and accelerating forces have to be absorbed. The main photo shows a perfect schuss

SNOWPLOUGH

The skier at left demonstrates the leg movement from the parallel position to the snowplough glide position. The photo sequence demonstrates that to turn left you put pressure on the right ski by leaning over it. This pushes the tail of the ski around on its inside edge. The narrower the snowplough the more you can edge the outside ski by pressing the knee inwards. This reduces skidding. Repeat the exercise in the other direction

high to improve your balance, and vice-versa.

To practise the schuss, select a gentle slope with a smooth transition from the level to the slope and to the level again. Try it several times in a wide stance. Try balancing exercises while schussing, such as bending your knees and touching your bindings, pushing with your poles, lifting one ski then the other and jumping.

To make a snowplough push the tails of the skis apart. The skis then skid on their inner edges. You push the skis out and the snow pushes them back – it all adds up to good balance. Practise mobility in the snowplough position. Vary the edging of the skis and the width of the plough to improve control. Use the plough as a brake, first by making it wider, then by using more edge.

Practise skidding too. Put greater weight on one ski and it will skid in a slight curve. Put weight on the ski and edge it more and you will turn; this is the snowplough turn. Weight and edge the skis alternately and you'll skid less and ski more on the edges.

Ski in a narrower plough with alternate changes of weighting and edging and you are starting to 'snowplough wedel'. In summary: wide plough = skid; narrow plough = carve; your speed will decide which.

BASIC SKILLS: GETTING UP, SIDE-STEP, HERRINGBONE

Falling over is part and parcel of skiing, and when it happens you just have to get up again! To stand up on level ground, put your skis together and draw your legs up to your body. Dig the edges in and, supporting yourself on one or both sticks, push yourself up, straightening your hips and knees.

On a slope your skis must, of course, be on your downhill side and at right angles to the fall-line. Set the uphill edges into the snow and push yourself up using your uphill arm.

To walk on skis on level ground, slide one ski forward then the other without lifting them from the ground, while pushing with the opposite stick. To make a gradual turn, move the front of one ski to one side and bring the other ski parallel.

No matter how good the lift system is, you will always need to do some walking uphill. Stand at the foot of a slope with your skis across the fall-line then step to the side with the uphill ski. Continue side-stepping uphill, keeping the skis parallel all the time and pushing the knees into the hill to edge the skis and prevent slipping.

To climb gentler slopes more quickly, use the herringbone step. Stand facing the hill with your ski tips apart to form a wide 'V'. Push your sticks behind you for support and take small steps up the hill, pressing your knees inwards to help the inside edges grip.

THE KICK TURN

At some point you will need to turn round on the spot instead of in a wide arc and to do this you need to learn the kick turn. Stand with your skis together (across the fall-line if you are on a slope) and turn your body through 90° to face downhill. Plant both sticks behind you, one at each end of the uphill ski, then kick the lower ski upright and rest it on its tail. Swing it round until it points in the opposite direction, then put your weight on it and bring the other ski around.

GETTING UP FROM A FALL

Getting up involves bending and stretching. Draw the legs up towards the body, keeping the skis across the fall-line if you are on a slope. Push yourself up with your hand or with your sticks, and straighten your legs into a standing position

HERRINGBONE STEP

Use the herringbone to walk up the fall-line. Place the ski tips wide apart and take small steps uphill without pausing in between or you will slip back. Plant your sticks behind you

SIDE-STEP

Step forward and sideways with the uphill ski and set its uphill edge, then bring the other ski parallel, planting your skis as you go. Small steps help prevent slipping

TRAVERSING

Traversing involves skiing across the slope on the uphill edges of the skis. The steeper the slope, the more you must edge the skis. Start with the skis apart to make it easier to press your knees into the hill. Edge the downhill ski particularly well as this is taking most of the weight. Your upper body should maintain a position facing slightly down the slope

BASIC SKILLS: TRAVERSE AND SIDE-SLIP

Traversing is moving across the slope on the uphill edges of your skis. Traverse with the skis slightly apart, the uphill ski a little in front of the downhill. If you find you are slipping sideways, press your knees more into the hill to make the edges grip. Practise several times, lifting the uphill ski occasionally as if you are going to step uphill. Try stepping down as well, but keep the edges well set to prevent yourself slipping.

COORDINATED MOVEMENT

Try traversing over small bumps too. You'll have to absorb the bumps by bending and stretching, while moving the knees into and away from the hill. As you will discover when we come to the swing later, the amount of weighting and edging have to correspond with each other and this coordination introduces another skill that has to be learned.

To stop in the traverse, turn the lower ski into the hill, sliding the uphill ski after it. This is the side-slip.

Now try it a bit faster and turn both skis into the hill at the same time, bending the legs first then straightening them as you turn. To start the turn, flatten the skis, then edge them again to exert control. The art of mastering this swing to the hill is found in the alternation between increasing and reducing the amount of edging.

HOW TO SKI GARLANDS

In the traverse, open the uphill ski into a plough and turn towards the fall-line. You will then gain speed, so swing the uphill ski parallel again in the side-slip and swing to the hill. If you repeat this movement you are skiing garlands — an excellent way of losing height on a traverse without crossing the fall-line. Practise with rhythmic movements and you'll be doing useful preparation for parallel turns. Make the plough less pronounced each time and turn more smoothly into the hill. Again, you are moving from skidding to carving and therefore practising for what comes later.

Be flexible. Make skating steps uphill as you traverse so as to practise the edging and thrust-off so important to the step swings you will learn later on.

TRAVERSING OVER BUMPS

This makes edging more difficult since the weighting varies as you go over the bumps and so the edging has to be varied accordingly. Bend and straighten your legs, shift your weight forwards or backwards and vary the amount of edging. All your movements need to work together to achieve total coordination

SIDE-SLIP

Starting in the traverse position, reduce the amount of edging to start side-slipping. Variation of this edging gives you control of the skis during the slide. The flatter the skis the faster you slide. To gain confidence, try starting the side-slip on a steeper slope and with a steeper incline. Step from the traverse into the side-slip. Then turn both skis at the same time, first open then closed. Practise in both directions

SKI LIFTS: HOW TO USE THEM

Ski lifts and cable cars are a boon to all skiers as they preserve energy for the descent. There are four main types of lift: T-bars, for one or two people; chair lifts for two or three people; bubble cars for four to six people; and cable cars, which range in capacity from 20 people to 100 or more. The key element with all lifts is knowing how to use them safely and efficiently. This chapter concentrates on these important factors.

Of about 22,000 lifts and cable cars throughout the world, roughly 13,000 are in Europe. Austria accounts for 4050 of these, of which 3400 are T-bar lifts, 500 are chairlifts and 150 are cable cars. The boom in lift systems is unmistakeable; between 1975 and 1985 the total number of lifts increased by about 50 per cent, while the number of people carried grew by about 150 per cent in the same period. This shows that the increase in traffic is due more to the improved performance of existing systems than the opening of new ones.

CODE OF SAFETY ON T-BARS
- Queuing. Always queue properly, in twos for T-bar lifts, to avoid unnecessary delays. Check whether the lift is attended or self-service; you are only allowed to grab the T-bar yourself on lifts that are designated self-service.
- Getting on. Step smartly into position and place both sticks in one hand. Look over your shoulder on your partner's side so that you can grab the bar with your free hand. Make sure your skis are properly aligned in the direction of travel before you move off.
- Moving off. Don't sit down on the bar but lean back gently and let it pull you, keeping your knees flexed to absorb any sudden movement. Shuffling steps help to make the start easier. At this moment it is even more important to control the direction of your skis on the track.
- Riding the lift. Keep your skis slightly apart and equally weighted. Don't lean outwards or against your partner in case you lose balance.

T-BAR LIFT

Queue properly. Hold your sticks in one hand away from the bar. Don't sit down but let the bar gently pull you. Weight your skis equally and stay in the track. If you fall, clear the tracks immediately. Take care when you get off, let go of the bar and leave the exit area quickly. If you are a beginner there is always a moment of trepidation the first time you go on a T-bar. The essential thing to remember is not to sit back on the bar, because it is simply not made to hold you in position. Just stand with knees slightly flexed in good balance and let the T-bar pull you gently along

- Keep to the track. Stay in the track, don't 'slalom' and don't leave the lift until you reach the top, otherwise you may endanger others.
- What to do if you fall. If you fall, make every effort to leave the track immediately, otherwise the people behind will have little chance of avoiding you.
- Preparing to leave the lift. Be ready in good time to release the lift. Push the bar away carefully, making sure it is not caught in your clothing before you let go.
- Getting off. Leave the lift quickly. Let go of the bar gently, don't carelessly throw it aside.
- Leaving the lift area. Leave the lift exit area immediately so as to make way for the people behind and avoid collisions or being struck by a swinging lift bar.

CODE OF SAFETY ON CHAIRLIFTS
- Queue properly and obey instructions. Queue in an orderly manner, without jostling. Observe the instructions of the lift attendants and ski patrol members, both at the lift and in the queuing area. Warn the attendant in good time if you are carrying children or are injured or disabled in any way.
- Once you have sat down on the chair, close the safety bar and keep your skis still on the foot rest. Kicking the skis together could release a binding.
- Don't swing the chair.
- Keep the skis and sticks pointing forwards.
- Observe No Smoking signs. Cigarettes can cause forest fires and endanger the lives of others.
- Never jump off or climb out.
- Remain seated until you reach the top of the lift. Remember that the drop to the snow below is always more dangerous than it appears.
- Before finally arriving at the top, open the safety bar and raise your ski tips.
- Leave the lift and exit area quickly in the direction indicated to avoid the risk of collisions.

CABLE CAR

Fasten your skis together with ski stoppers and scrape any snow off your boots. Queue in an orderly manner without jostling. If numbers are excessive, use other lifts

CHAIRLIFT

Queue properly. Close the safety bar and put your skis on the foot rest. Don't swing, smoke or jump off. At the top, open the safety bar and lift your ski tips. Get off promptly and leave the exit area immediately

SWING TO THE HILL

Once you've mastered this basic swing, start from a steeper angle each time. The faster you go, the easier the turn. At higher speeds, turn more on the edges – carve the turn. As you approach the turn, bend your legs and hips then straighten them to swing round. Plant the inner pole to begin the turn. Swing around ridges or bumps. Try to swing smoothly every time and, above all, practise the swing both ways

SWING TO THE HILL

When you turned the skis from the traverse into the side-slip you made your first swing to the hill. Now let's swing away from the fall-line until you come to a stop. (The fall-line is an imaginary line which follows the steepest line of descent down the slope.)

Start off in a schuss, with the skis parallel. As you gain speed bend the knees, then stretch and turn the legs bringing the skis around.

Try to make as smooth a swing as possible. When travelling faster or from a steeper angle, you'll find your skis edge more easily and thus require less effort from your legs.

Practise the swing to the hill by turning and side-slipping around the back of small bumps. You'll find that bumps reduce the snow resistance and help you make the turn.

Vary the speed and radius of the turn and try it out in slightly deeper snow. Approach the turn faster so the momentum helps you. Weight the inside ski in order to control its rotation, but more than half of the weight should be on the outside ski.

In any swing, 60% of the movement is the swing to the hill so it is important that you learn all of its variations. Practise in both directions working on your weak side most often.

Your ski teacher will set up slalom gates for you to swing around. This will be a new feeling but a discipline that will eventually bring you greater freedom when skiing the different types of terrain.

If you suddenly see an obstruction or another skier in your way you will want to stop quickly. Learn how to turn your skis sideways suddenly from the schuss position in the manner an ice-hockey player stops (it is sometimes called the hockey stop). Plant your stick and quickly turn your skis at right angles to the direction of travel. Weight the inner ski as well but not too much, otherwise you may catch an edge. Here again, practise turning both ways; other skiers won't be looking for your 'good side'.

Having mastered the schuss, the traverse, the snowplough, the swing to the hill and the emergency stop, you are ready for the terrain. Off you go then, but follow your instructor. Turning on gentle slopes, traversing the steeper ones, side-slipping and making garlands on the slopes in between should be the plan. Increase your speed and you'll turn more smoothly.

Practise the snowplough on gentler slopes again and again. Take the risk of stepping towards, and later against, the outer ski – this is the pedal wedeln. Without thinking, you'll begin to bring the inner ski parallel as you turn.

As soon as you start skiing snowplough turns on steeper slopes, your skis will run away from you, so bring the inner ski into line with the outer one and put weight on it. You know from the hockey stop that this is a good brake. Do this consciously on every turn and you are starting to 'swing', the subject of the following section.

EMERGENCY STOP

Suddenly you may see an obstacle in your path. To stop, immediately plant both skis across the direction of travel. It is made easier by drawing the legs up momentarily to unweight the skis. It is essential that you practise this stop in both directions – you can't be choosy in an emergency!

HOW THE SKIS TURN

When you gain an understanding of how and why skis turn, you are on your way to unlocking the door to successful skiing. This section deals mainly with how the skis turn; the 'why' is dealt with in detail in the chapter entitled 'The Swing'.

We have two main types of forces which we can harness to help us turn (swing) our skis. On the one hand we have the muscular forces, and on the other, forces such as gravity, weight, centrifuge, momentum and snow resistance. The good skier uses his muscular power to make these external forces work for him.

Upon turning the skis the body is pushed outwards by centrifugal force. To counteract this, the skier leans into the curve and sets the edges of the skis into the snow to increase grip.

This is a complex subject, but let us try and reduce it to its essentials and see how, in practice, the skier can apply the principles in order to improve his technique.

Modern skis are made so that they bend under pressure. They are also waisted, i.e. narrower in the middle and wider at the tips and base. When pressure is applied to skis in the turn, they will do one of two things: they will skid or they will carve. The skis skid at low speed, if the angle of the base of the skis is flat to the snow. But if the skis are put on their edges at higher speed, they will form an arc and glide along that arc. This is known as carving.

Ideally you should always try to 'carve' the turn, because it is more economical, generates more momentum and makes it easier to swing from one counteracting force to the next. In practice, however, most edged skis have a degree of skidding in them. Indeed, there are times when it is better to skid, but there are also times when carving is essential – an emergency stop, for example, needs extreme pressure.

The initiation of the turn always requires a change of weight and pressure from the outside ski of one turn to the outside ski of the next turn. Problems begin when one or both skis are weighted too much at the tip or tail of the ski. If you step hard onto the inner ski, it edges and grips better. If the pressure is too great, however, the edge will catch. Thus, the interplay is clear: step onto the outer ski and it starts to swing around; step onto the inner ski and it grips and steers better.

To steer the swing, the weight is maintained two-thirds on the downhill ski and one-third on the uphill ski. This gives a good plaform to thrust off for the next swing. In reality we are continually changing and adapting the degree of weighting to suit the conditions.

Bumps make swinging (turning) easier, since the skis pivot around their centre, but better steering and balance is required. Speed has the effect of making swinging easier but the steering becomes harder. With deep snow it is the other way round: easier steering and harder swinging.

In summary: the forces generated when swinging perform the main work, while our muscle-power is used to distribute pressure and weight. When we learn to swing with good technique we have a great deal of power under our control.

FORCES IN ACTION

Strong forces act upon the body in skiing. At high speeds these can be up to four times the body weight, so racing skiers in particular need strong legs. A waisted ski with enough weight on it to make it bend would travel in a curve anyway. If, in addition, it is placed at an angle to the direction of travel it will also turn according to the distribution of the weight. The edged and weighted part of the ski will grip better. In simple terms: the swing pushes the body outwards (100% arrow), the snow offers resistance via the edges (60%/ 40% arrows – above). These forces combine to produce the important inward lean

INWARD LEAN

The inward lean of the skier is determined by the speed and radius of the turn. If he leans into the swing, the inside ski will grip well; if he leans too far, the skis will slip as racers tend to do. If you put too much weight on the outside ski, it flattens and skids away. The skier in the picture is on his outside ski. To start the ski turning, it is unweighted and to continue turning it is weighted again. This alternation of pressure is for effective swinging

100%

100%

SKIDDING AND CARVING COMPARED

Control of the skis is determined by the skier's ability. Ability determines speed and this in turn differentiates between skidding and carving.

As mentioned in the previous chapter, pressure applied to skis which are flat to the snow causes them to skid during the swing. But if strong pressure is applied at speed, the skis can be put on their edges, increasing control and momentum, and this is called carving.

In the 'carved' swing you feel as though your skis are on a set of rails and the momentum is pulling you around, as you lean into the swing. The carved skis give a good grip, and this enables you to thrust off for the next swing. Skidded skis give little grip to start the next swing and require more balancing, which prevents controlled turning (swinging).

The faster you ski, the more you need to lean into the curve while keeping your balance. This increases the action of centrifugal force, which acts more in a diagonal direction on the body, which in turn is counteracted by the snow pressing against the skis' edges. Because of this there is a longer base over which the body weight can be shifted back and forth and a safer support from which to thrust off or bank the

body downhill and into the swing.

If skiing slowly you have to place most of your weight on the outer ski in order to start skidding. You 'step across' always from the inside to the outside ski. When steering, the inside ski is also weighted slightly. As you go faster the skidding skis will begin to clatter.

As you increase speed you'll have to put some weight on the inside ski soon after starting to swing, which is why you lean into the swing with your upper body facing towards the valley. If you lean too soon or too far, the inside ski will open into the scissors position, causing it to skid and brake.

Carving can only be done perfectly with parallel skis; in the stem and scissors one ski will always be skidding. When we refer to carving we usually mean 'skidding as little as possible'. Racing skiers strive towards perfect carving — 'gliding on the entire arc of the inside edge' — but less experienced skiers learn by increasing their speed to progress from skidding to carving within each type of swing.

In summary then: the more you learn to carve the skis, the better will be your control and momentum and your ability to create a series of linked swings. Remember that most carved swings have a degree of skid in them, but the more you strive to eliminate the skidding element the more energy you will conserve, the more you will control the swing, and the more momentum and rhythm will be developed.

SKIDDING, CARVING

The top row of pictures illustrate skidding and the bottom row carving

CARVING OLD AND NEW

The distinctive narrow track of the modern carved skis is seen at left. In the 1950s, however, speeds were lower, pistes were softer and there were few bumps. Long, rigid wooden skis (below) had to be unweighted with a jump to turn them

43

THE KEY TO SUCCESSFUL SKIING

The term 'schwingen' occupies a very special place in the vocabulary of Austrian skiing. Schwingen literally means to swing. Just as a conductor swings his baton to control and bring out the best sound possible from his orchestra, so the skier needs to combine tempo, rhythm, balance, momentum, and sheer exuberance to perfect his skiing skills. That's why 'swinging' is a much better word than 'turning' to describe the skier's linked movements as he descends the mountain — and why we use 'swing' and 'swinging' to convey all the dynamics and effectiveness of this key element of technique. A perfect example of linked swings is shown in the photograph opposite.

The inner core of the swing is the moment when the change of direction takes place, i.e. from one direction into the opposite one. It is at this point that the skier does the real work. He uses his muscular forces and the momentum generated by transferring the pressure and weighting from the outside ski of one swing, to the outside ski of the next. The weight transfer is at times combined with a vertical weight shift (unweighting) or with a fore and aft weight shift. These differentiations are never 'black and white', but more like shades of grey.

The swing could thus be categorized as swinging with a greater or lesser shift of weight. This can't be seen, but only felt.

The clear aim nowadays is to become the 'complete skier', so that you can tackle all types of terrain in safety and with enjoyment and move up the experience curve to the perfection of technique. The route to this objective is through the eight swings of the Austrian method:

Stem swing, opening the uphill/downhill ski
Parallel swing, opening the uphill/downhill ski
Parallel swing with up/down unweighting
Scissors swing opening the uphill/downhill ski

These eight swings provide the key to skiing in all situations.

On the following pages we examine them in detail. Once you have got the hang of it, try not to think in terms of categories. In all types of swinging there is an unbroken progression from uphill to downhill opening of the ski.

As a preliminary to a detailed examination of each swing, we start with a schematic presentation in which we have selected two photographs per swing (with inset diagram). They show the relationship of each swing, the critical position of the skis at the moment the swing is initiated, where weight is placed and how it is transferred to complete the swing ready to start the next one.

The black skis in the diagrams take two-thirds of the skier's weight and the red skis one third. The broken line shows the path of travel and the arrow shows the direction of weight-shift. The diagram accompanying the caption shows the point along the path of travel at which each swing is initiated.

EIGHT STEPS TO A PERFECT TECHNIQUE

In this book, we refer to the uphill, downhill, inside and outside ski. These terms are applied to the ski according to its position on the path of travel at a given moment. Thus, in the steering phase of a swing, the uphill (or inside) ski is the ski nearest to

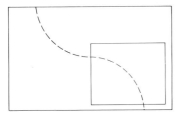

1 STEM SWING, OPENING THE UPHILL SKI

- From the traverse or previous swing, stem out the uphill ski
- Turn stem towards fall-line
- Plant stick in fall-line
- Thrust off from inside ski
Step towards outside ski
- Bring inside ski parallel
- Steer to the hill

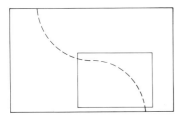

2 STEM SWING, OPENING THE DOWNHILL SKI

- The pressure from the previous steering opens the downhill (outside) ski into a stem
- Edge the downhill ski firmly to get a good hold
- Plant stick and thrust off from the hold of the downhill ski
- Bank into the swing while bringing the inside ski parallel
- Steer to the hill

the hill. It becomes the outside ski as a new swing is initiated and the downhill ski in the steer to the hill as the fall line is crossed. The ski furthest from the hill is the downhill (or outside) ski. It becomes the inside ski during the swing and the new uphill (or inside) ski in the steer to the hill. And vice versa for the next swing. The diagrams of the eight key swings show how this happens.

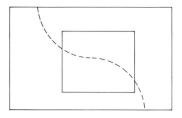

3 PARALLEL SWING, OPENING THE UPHILL SKI

- From the traverse or end of the swing, open the uphill ski but keep it parallel
- Plant stick, thrust off from outside (downhill) ski
- Change edge of new outside ski, weight it and swing it
- Bring inside ski parallel
- Bank into the swing
- Steer to the hill

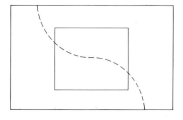

4 PARALLEL SWING, OPENING THE DOWNHILL SKI

- From the end of the swing, the pressure opens the downhill ski
- Plant stick
- Bend inside leg whilst straightening outside leg
- Bank body downhill
- Bring inside ski parallel
- Steer to the hill

EIGHT STEPS TO A PERFECT TECHNIQUE

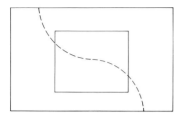

5 PARALLEL SWING, WITH UP-UNWEIGHTING

- At the end of the swing, bend knees to weight both skis
- Plant stick
- Rise up with both legs to unweight the skis
- Swing the unweighted skis
- Continue swinging as the pressure on skis and body builds up again
- Steer to the hill

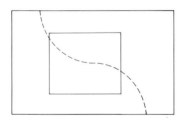

6 PARALLEL SWING, WITH DOWN-UNWEIGHTING

- At the end of the swing, let legs bend under pressure
- Plant stick
- Change edges with legs bent
- Bank body downhill
- Straighten and swing legs
- Steer to the hill

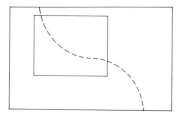

7 SCISSORS SWING, OPENING THE UPHILL SKI

- At the end of the swing, edge the downhill ski well
- Thrust off from downhill ski
- Put uphill ski in a scissors position, weight it and swing it. Plant stick
- Bank body downhill
- Bring inside ski parallel
- Steer to the hill

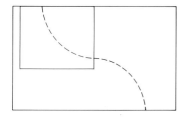

8 SCISSORS SWING, OPENING THE DOWNHILL SKI

- At the end of the swing, the pressure of the steering opens the skis into a scissors position
- Unweight downhill ski which becomes inside ski, stretch uphill leg
- Plant stick
- Bank body downhill
- Bring inside ski parallel
- Steer to the hill

STEM SWING, OPENING THE UPHILL SKI

On pages 30-31 we explained the snowplough turn. A few of them are bound to have gone wrong because your plough was too narrow, the skis were not edged enough or you leaned back too far. Instinctively you'll have brought the inside ski around to skid and brake and turn both skis skidding to the hill.

Now use this experience for the stem swing, opening the uphill ski, which is also called the uphill stem. Choose a flattish slope and turn towards the fall-line in a plough (stem). Plant the inside stick and bring the inside ski parallel. For the next swing, stem the uphill ski out again.

A VERSATILE TECHNIQUE
The circumstances will determine how wide you open the skis, how hard you edge them in the stem, how long you turn in the stem and how energetically you bring the inside ski round. The uphill stem is so adaptable it can work everywhere for everyone. Try some variations.

Increase your speed and you'll find that you'll open the skis less, swing earlier and raise your body less in the swing. This is called stem stepping.

When opening the uphill ski, you'll find that the downhill ski starts to slip away so you must quickly thrust off from it. You are beginning to make the stem with the downhill ski.

On averagely steep slopes you will have to stem wider and for longer and to swing later. Avoid icy slopes as these can easily cause you to start to skid as you bring the inside ski around.

Make shorter swings too. When you do so you'll have less time to open the uphill ski and will increasingly open both skis and have to thrust off more from the inside ski.

You can also try the stem swing over bumps. Open the uphill ski and you ride onto the bump, plant the inside stick and turn the inside ski on the top of the bump. To start with, traverse between the swings, and when you have regained your balance, open the skis for the next swing. You'll soon become confident enough to swing on any bump and will hardly have time to open the uphill ski: you'll open both skis sometimes, the downhill even more.

AROUND THE GATES
Don't be put off when your ski teacher sets up slalom gates. They will be far enough apart for you to ski individual swings. As soon as he places them closer together, however, you'll have to link your swings closer and closer. The pressure on the downhill ski will increase and force it to stem — and that's the downhill stem. Initially you'll lift your body more in the swing, but by the time you are swinging both skis in one movement you'll be well on the way to mastering it.

TECHNIQUE SEQUENCE

From the traverse or the end of the last swing, open the uphill ski into the stem (rear view far left). Turn the stem towards the fall-line (rear view left). In or before the fall-line, close the inside ski to side-slip — swing! Plant the inside stick to help you swing. Steer to the hill

STEM SWINGS OVER BUMPS

Approach the bump from the traverse. On the rising side, stem the uphill ski. On the top of the bump, bring the inside ski parallel to side-slip. Traverse a little before the next swing

STEM SWING, OPENING THE DOWNHILL SKI

This swing is also called the downhill stem. The faster you ski, the less time you have in which to open the uphill ski. Instead, simply open and weight the downhill ski and thrust off from it, swinging both skis beyond the fall-line. For the thrust-off, plant the downhill stick for support and raise your body slightly if you need to.

This requires finer balance and greater courage, but soon you will be able to weight the downhill ski more precisely and the thrust-off will be more economical – your upper body will remain 'quieter'. It's not the wideness of a downhill stem that matters; the essential point is the grip for the thrust-off or the thrust-off itself. If the downhill ski slips away when weighted, balancing becomes difficult and hinders a controlled swing; your legs become tense and are unable to turn the skis smoothly. The pelvis and upper body must swing with the legs. For steering you then stand in a rotated position over the skis. Ski more and more from the legs.

SWING VARIATIONS
Vary the speed and length of the swings. The higher the speed, the easier the swing will be, especially on smooth slopes. Your movement will become more economical, you'll put pressure, less sideways and more downward, onto the outside ski – this reduces skidding and you'll begin to carve.

Short swings are easier to link together. If you traverse between swings you have to stem the downhill ski every time. Apply pressure optimally to the outside ski so that you can thrust off from it. Go down a little lower before the thrust-off so as to increase the pressure and thus the grip of the downhill ski.

Gradually try steeper slopes, but always look for good snow which the skis can grip. On ice your skis will slide no matter how much you weight them and you'll be too busy balancing to swing. Initially on steeper slopes, it is therefore a good idea to make individual swings in order to restore your balance and confidence for the next one.

Over bumps the uphill side of the bump will give your downhill ski a good hold without the need for much edging. Nor do you need to up-unweight – the skis swing around so easily.

Find a smoother slope again to practise rhythmic swings. You will hardly leave the plough position but you'll swing quickly to and fro. This is known as the plough wedeln.

SLALOM GATES AGAIN
This time your teacher will place the gates nearer the fall-line. Don't think too much about your movements, just concentrate on getting round the next gate as quickly as possible.

The placing of the gates will vary. For wide placing ski slowly and open the uphill ski. For narrow placing ski faster and open the downhill ski.

When skiing alone, perform a mixture of uphill and downhill stems. Switch as often as you can for this will help you develop adaptability and fluency in your skiing. Each swing is appropriate to a specific situation – and variety will sustain your interest.

TECHNIQUE

The downhill stem – the stem swing opening the downhill ski – requires greater sensitivity and balance. Good edging of the downhill ski makes for good grip from which you can thrust off well and swing both skis in one motion. The downhill ski must not only be edged, but also weighted. Merely straightening the downhill leg causes skidding

SEQUENCE

The pressure from the previous steering opens the downhill ski into a stem. Edge the downhill ski firmly to get a good grip (rear view bottom left). Plant stick and thrust off from the grip of the downhill ski (rear view top left). Bank into the swing while bringing the inside ski parallel. Steer to the hill

PARALLEL SWING, OPENING THE UPHILL SKI

By now you'll be stemming with the uphill ski more confidently, and opening it parallel more often. It is time, therefore, to go on to the parallel swing, opening the uphill ski. This version is also known as the parallel step turn.

Start at a slow speed by placing the uphill ski clearly to the side and on its inside edge. Soon you'll be placing it flat and, as you increase speed, you'll no longer need to open it wide and will place it on its uphill edge.

Initially, then, you change the edge while the ski is off the ground; later on you change the edges on the snow when you have worked up sufficient speed.

To start with you'll find that you lift your body in the swing and even rotate it with the outside ski, but as you get better

TECHNIQUE SEQUENCE

From the traverse, move uphill
ski sideways and keep parallel to
the downhill ski
Set uphill ski on inside edge at
first, then flat and finally on uphill
edge
Thrust off from downhill ski
and start uphill ski turning
Plant inside stick on thrust-off,
swing skis past the fall-line
In practice, increase speed with
shorter swings, and make less
and less lateral movement
of the skis

Parallel Swing, Opening the Uphill Ski (continued)
you'll be opening, edging and swinging as required. Your body will remain 'quieter', less active, and you'll be swinging the skis with your legs only.

As this swinging technique becomes a matter of routine, you'll ski faster and with greater ease. You'll notice that the pressure of steering forces you into a wider stance and you no longer need to open the skis. All you do to initiate the swing is lift the downhill ski, and the momentum then draws your body across the tip of the ski to the downhill side. You will then bank from one side to the other like a motorcyclist, and this requires good balance.

Experiment on steeper slopes. At first you'll set the uphill ski on its inside edge again, but soon you will be swinging rhythmically and setting the outside edge more often. The moment you reach flatter terrain, the pressure will open the skis for you. Vary the speed, but don't forget the rhythm!

Steer the skis round when swinging, using less and less lateral movement. Edge the outside ski sooner and to a greater extent. The tail of the outside ski will swing less outwards. The tip will turn more into the swing and you will carve the skis.

The faster and more relaxed and rhythmically you ski, the more you can weight the inside ski. The skis then open easily into the scissors position. When this happens you are doing the scissors swing.

Swing over the bumps. Don't push the uphill ski too far out, because the bumps make it easier to pivot anyway. Soon you'll be skiing parallel, opening the downhill ski.

Again you will practise with slalom gates. If they are widely spaced, open the uphill ski in a stem or parallel position. The moment the movement becomes rhythmical, however, it pushes your downhill ski into the stem or parallel position. Good balance is essential. It won't be long before you'll be aware of just how much slalom gates can improve technique.

Try the manoeuvre out in fresh snow on a hard base. Pay particular attention to good steering; the inside ski especially can only be steered if it is sensitively weighted.

You have now learned three ways to swing. Use them all and vary the speed and radius each time. It will help you become more fluent and will make skiing more fun.

FRONT VIEW

Push the uphill ski out to the side. If you lack sufficient speed the outside ski can be turned with the hips. This anticipates the initiation of the swing so that you are fully prepared to execute it properly. Plant stick to help balance and as support for the turn

57

PARALLEL SWING, OPENING THE DOWNHILL SKI

In the downhill stem, explained on pages 52 and 53, we pointed out that the more relaxed, confident, energetic and rhythmic your swings, the less time you had to open the uphill ski. Steering pushed your skis apart. From this position you swung, while unweighting the downhill ski (which became the inside ski during the swing). In doing this, you bent the inside leg and straightened the outside leg – known as pedalling.

For the parallel swing opening the downhill ski, we have to consciously bend the inside leg and straighten the outside leg. The upper body will then be pushed naturally across the ski tips. Bank into the turn and bring the inside ski parallel. Steer to the hill by leaning the body inwards instead of pushing the legs outwards.

TECHNIQUE SEQUENCE

Ski faster and swing more
rhythmically nearer to the fall-
line. Steering forces the skis into
a wider track. Bend the inside leg
to unweight the inside ski while
straightening the outside leg.
Bank the body downhill over the
ski tips and bring the inside ski
parallel. Steer to the hill

Parallel Swing, Opening the Downhill Ski (continued)

Now ski with faster, shorter, more rhythmical swings. Begin with a slight to moderate slope to start with. The faster you ski, the more you have to weight the inside ski as well, and the more easily you'll take up the scissors position. Be careful, though; the inside ski can easily carve the wrong line when weighted.

Change the rhythm and thus the type of swing. Whether stemming or parallel, your ability and the particular situation will decide whether you open the uphill ski or the momentum pushes your skis apart.

Skiing over different terrain helps you become more versatile. Consciously vary the type of swing, changing from skidding to carving and back again, but always keep to the appropriate speed of course.

Also perform parallel swings in light fresh snow, but with carefully measured weight shifts. If you unweight the inside ski completely for too long, the resistance of the snow will force it sideways.

When skiing over bumps you'll hardly have time to open uphill. 'A turn for every bump' results in swinging with downhill opening, in which the bump pushes the downhill ski into a wider track.

Your ski teacher will set up slalom gates again, initially with a greater offset from the fall-line so you can repeat the parallel swing opening the uphill ski. When the gates are positioned nearer the fall-line you can practise swinging by opening the downhill ski.

BANKING THE BODY

The two skiers in the photograph above are clearly banking into the swing. Good balance is required for this to be effectively executed and this lean is easier to see at higher speeds. In this photogragh the skiers are skiing in 'practice deep snow'

To summarize then: for slower skiing, individual turns, steeper slopes and more difficult terrain, use either the stem swing opening the uphill ski or the parallel swing opening the uphill ski. For faster, more rhythmic skiing on less steep slopes or where turning is easier use the stem swing opening the downhill ski or the parallel swing opening the downhill ski.

FRONT VIEW

Weighting the inside ski makes it possible to open the downhill ski (right). You can now swing at low speed by turning the pelvis with the thrust off from the downhill ski. The downhill leg turns the toe in more, which aids this thrust-off. The stick should never be planted too far to the side, otherwise you tend to turn with the pelvis to compensate

REAR VIEW

Plant stick. Bend the inside leg while straightening the outside leg, which increases the pressure on the outside ski (bottom left). Bank the body downhill whilst bringing the inside ski parallel (bottom right)

PARALLEL SWING WITH UP-UNWEIGHTING

No matter how much fitness training you have done, you'll find that parallel swinging with unweighting requires strong legs and will take a little time to master, but it will be worthwhile.

From the traverse, bend your knees and turn the skis slightly to the hill; or, if steering, let the pressure bend your legs. Thrust off from the edges with both legs, planting the inside pole for support. As your legs straighten, rotate legs and skis under your body and continue turning the skis as smoothly as possible as you land. The smoother the thrust-off and landing, the smoother you will swing the skis. Practise steering smooth curves.

In parallel swinging with up-unweighting you shift your weight sideways as you thrust off. This is especially apparent when you ski in a wider stance: you always thrust off slightly earlier and harder from the downhill ski which is weighted more.

Bear in mind that the more you unweight the skis the easier they will turn, but the more balance will be upset. After the thrust-off you momentarily 'lose grip', so it is important that the skis only leave the snow for a second and that you plant the inside stick as a 'temporary leg'.

At higher speeds you have to up-unweight more gently; the swinging motion will relieve you of some work and help turn the skis further. As you link the swings together, steering pressure and thrust-off will overlap and you'll begin to feel the rhythm of the movement.

The faster you swing, the less time you have to up-unweight, so your body remains 'quieter'. This doesn't matter, since the increasing edge set provides greater thrust. Practise at first on moderate slopes with good snow.

Vary the radius of the swings and thus the thrust-off and turn. Avoid icy slopes at all times, as you can easily slip on these when thrusting off.

When skiing over bumps, you don't need to unweight. The bumps do it for you! If you unweight as well, you'll take off and find it difficult to recover your momentum.

Your teacher will set up gates again. First they'll be offset sideways so that you have to thrust off and swing more strongly. Then they'll be nearer the fall-line, so that the up-unweighting is reduced and the legs swing the skis round from the waist down. As always, vary the swing when practising — sometimes up-unweighting, sometimes keeping the body still.

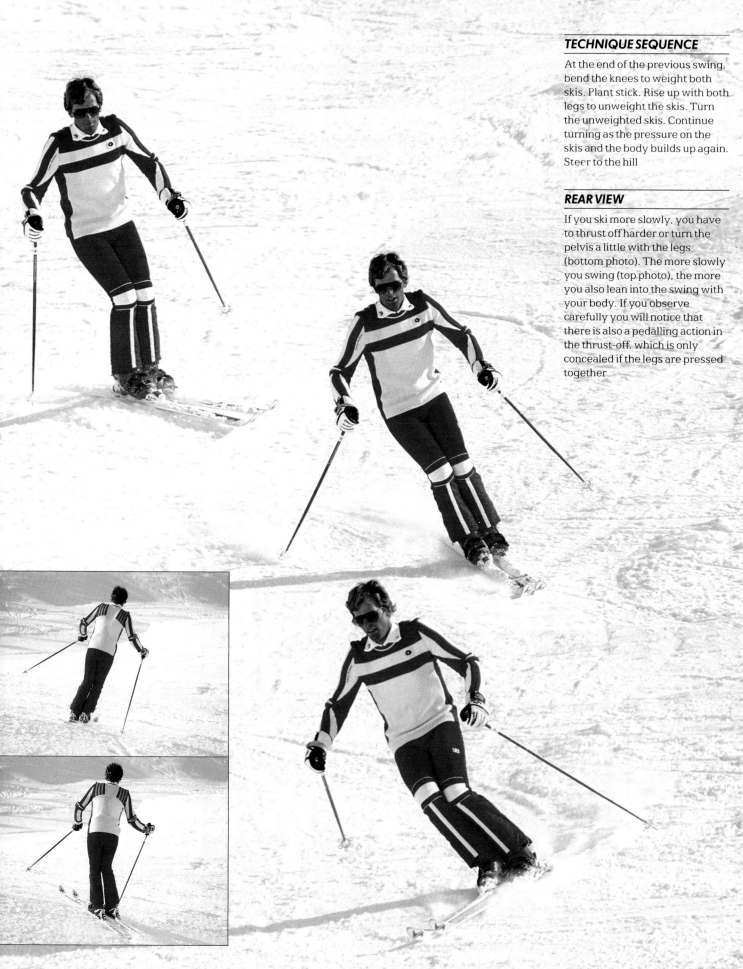

TECHNIQUE SEQUENCE

At the end of the previous swing, bend the knees to weight both skis. Plant stick. Rise up with both legs to unweight the skis. Turn the unweighted skis. Continue turning as the pressure on the skis and the body builds up again. Steer to the hill

REAR VIEW

If you ski more slowly, you have to thrust off harder or turn the pelvis a little with the legs (bottom photo). The more slowly you swing (top photo), the more you also lean into the swing with your body. If you observe carefully you will notice that there is also a pedalling action in the thrust-off, which is only concealed if the legs are pressed together

PARALLEL SWING WITH DOWN-UNWEIGHTING

The less up-unweighting you do, the more you have to bend and straighten your legs in order to change edges and swing the skis round.

As you come to the end of one swing, the pressure will concertina your legs. The more you bend your legs, the sooner the skis will glide forwards. While your legs are bent you have to change edges and then continue to swing as you straighten them.

Try swinging rhythmically straight away. Allow your legs to be bent, and straighten them when the skis are flat on the snow half way through the edge change. It will help enormously if you plant your stick when changing edges and swinging. You'll swing from thrust-off to thrust-off, i.e. swing and counterswing.

Coming out of the steering phase let your legs be bent under the pressure in one continuous movement. Plant stick. Change edges, with your legs bent. Bank your body downhill then straighten and swing your legs. Steer to the hill. Controlled bending and stretching results in smoother swings

65

Parallel Swing with Down-Unweighting (continued)

Do some single turns now. Start with a swing to the hill to bend your legs. The counter-swing should flow smoothly into the edge change and start of the next swing. This way you don't spend too long in a difficult crouch, and the tensing and relaxing of the muscles will alternate rhythmically. The legs do most of the work in balancing, swinging and steering, so keep the practice runs short to start with.

SMOOTH MOVEMENT

The more precise your bending and stretching movements, the more smoothly you'll swing. Keep close to the fall-line at first. It means you will not have to swing so far and you'll swing more smoothly and carve better.

Steeper slopes often force you to make single swings, with the risk of becoming tensed in the crouch position. If you sense this happening, it is better to turn with up-unweighting.

You'll have noticed by now that it is easy, and more fun, to swing on bumps. The bump will bend your legs, which can then pivot the skis on top of the bump and continue swinging and straightening on the downhill side. You can only swing quickly and with ease if your legs are relaxed and supple. Don't overdo the practice, however, as down-unweighting is more strenuous than up-unweighting.

Swing through the slalom gates, which should be placed close to the fall-line to keep your swings closely linked and prevent your muscles from becoming tense. If the gates are offset you'll have to swing by stepping or up-unweighting.

DEEP SNOW CONDITIONS

Swinging by bending and straightening the legs becomes easier in deep snow. Like the bumps and moguls, deep snow forces your legs to bend. As soon as the skis flatten in the edge change, you must straighten your legs and continue swinging round. Alternate rhythmically between bending and straightening your legs, planting the stick between the two movements, as you need a fixed point when you push your legs to the side and thus move out of balance.

In deep snow you can afford to lean further back to change edges. Don't be deceived though; relative to the surface of the snow you *are* leaning well back, but much less so in relation to the skis which sink in further at the tails.

You now have a whole variety of swings in your repertoire. Alternate between up and down unweighting with an occasional step swing thrown in for good measure. Use all the forms of swinging you have learned so far and always try to match the right speed to the right swing.

The much-vaunted difference between the old parallel swing and the step swing turns out to be very small in fact. For sharper swings you need more 'pedalling' and for gentler swings less. One-legged and two-legged skiing both have their uses.

SHIFTING WEIGHT

You will soon discover that, when skiing more slowly or making single turns, you have to open the uphill ski and shift the weight more consciously. When swinging faster and more rhythmically on the other hand, you shift your weight from the inside to the outside ski without having to think about it at all. With uphill opening you step; with downhill opening you bank. Use both methods when practising.

FRONT VIEW

Change edges with the legs bent. As the skis are pushed away to the side, move onto the edges (top). Careful extension of the legs produces smoother curves; sudden, strong extension causes slipping. Learn to stretch and turn with precision. It is particularly effective when skiing over bumps, as the skis remain in contact with the snow

EDGE CHANGING AND EXTENSION FROM THE BACK

If the edge change is too slow, the pelvis turns with the legs. Stick planting helps. Do not overdo the backward lean when changing edges, as it pushes the legs forward and accentuates the lean. In summary: weight the ski for steering; unweight the tips for edge change; planting the stick helps initiate the turn and arrests backward lean

THE SWING

THE WEDELN

If you have noticed what fun it is to swing your legs rhythmically to and fro from the hips, then you have already done the wedeln (German for tail-wagging).

Your legs swing from side to side. Whether your upper body remains still or moves up and down, will be decided by the circumstances. If swinging is difficult, up-unweighting makes it easier; in good conditions this won't be necessary, but practise between the two: more unweighting and you will skid more; less unweighting and you will carve better. Both are important. On concave paths (gunbarrels) and bottlenecks you will need to unweight; on smooth pistes it is unnecessary. Racing skiers use the wedeln through narrow slalom gates.

Vary the swings again. On steeper slopes you will turn well with up-unweighting and on flatter slopes you will glide well with a 'quiet' body. Practise braking and gliding on steep and shallow slopes.

Wedel in time with your ski teacher or a friend. Wedel through the hollows between the bumps where the ski tips won't flap up and down so much, but start each swing decisively.

Practise the wedeln without sticks, or in a low crouch position, or even on one leg. The wedeln is most challenging in deep snow, where weighting and unweighting merge most rhythmically one into the other.

Skiing through gates will help you to improve this movement. Your ski teacher will first set up the gates on a smooth slope with good grip, then will later place them closer together on a steeper slope.

On an icy surface, he will again set up easy gates, varying the lateral placement to suit the conditions.

Control your breathing to improve your technique. Breathing out loud will help. Breathe in when you are swinging or up-unweighting; breathe out when the body is under pressure when steering.

The wedeln is one of the most beautiful and satisfying movements. Get it right and you will experience one of the real joys of skiing.

TECHNIQUE SEQUENCE

Swing the legs from side to side under your body. Edge change is made easier if you support yourself on the inside stick, planting it close to the ski. Despite the weight shift, put some weight on the inside ski early on. If it is weighted too much, though, it will immediately stray into a scissors position. Practise the wedeln especially between bumps – strong legs are required! The wedeln is a very satisfying movement when performed fluently, and well worth mastering

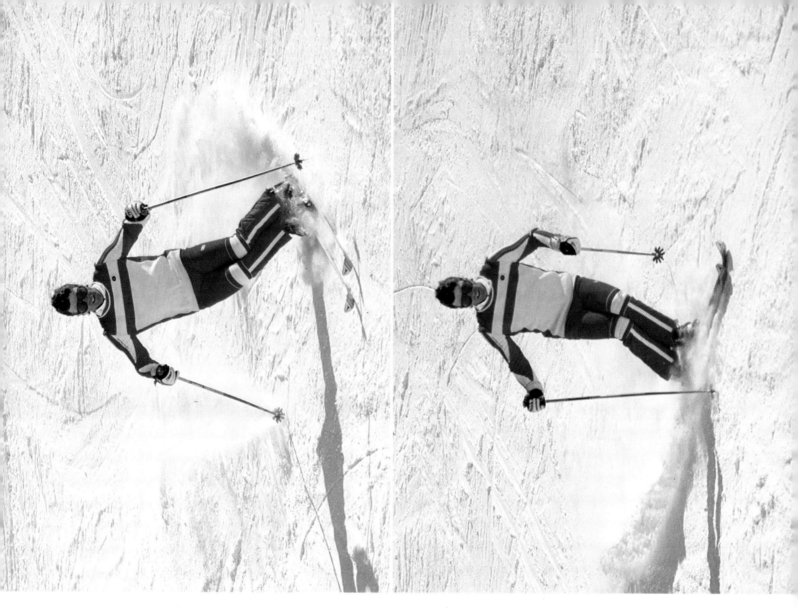

THE MIDDLE WAY

The skis swing rhythmically from one edge set to the next. If you are too upright, the pelvis has to turn with the legs. If the legs are bent too much, you are forced into a backward lean when changing edges, which is only accentuated if the legs are stretched again. So it is important to feel for a 'middle' position to achieve maximum effect

SCISSORS SWING, OPENING THE UPHILL SKI

You may not yet have learned the scissors swing but, without noticing it, you will have already moved the uphill ski into a scissors position many times.

When steering, guide the outside ski around on its edge to give a good support for the thrust-off. Thrust off diagonally forwards and push out the tip of the uphill ski into the scissors position. In thrusting off, your weight shifts over the new outside ski which you should turn before bringing the inside ski round. Plant the inside stick to help initiate the turn and to provide extra balance. You can lift your body a little on thrust-off, but not so much that it is completely straightened, otherwise you will have to rotate your hips as well, which adversely affects steering.

TECHNIQUE SEQUENCE

Steer to the end of a swing. Thrust off from the outside ski, pushing the uphill ski into the scissors. Plant the inside stick to initiate the swing of the outside ski, and bring the inside ski parallel. Steer to the end of the swing on the inside edges of the skis

Scissors Swing, Opening the Uphill Ski (continued)

LEGS AND HIPS

The main points to note are as follows: if you turn only your legs, place the skis on their edges during the swing. If you turn your hips as well, the skis require less edging. It follows that you can turn with the hips as far as the fall-line. The experts call this 'anticipation'. Beyond the fall-line (or just before it at high speed), you should turn only the legs, especially the outside leg.

If the skis are hard to turn but easy to steer, you can turn with the hips before the legs. If turning is easier and steering is harder, turn both the legs and the hips. If steering is difficult you should turn only the legs and not the hips.

The amount of edging and the amount of turning can thus be varied to suit the situation.

Your legs are not always turned in the same way. To skid, you push your heels outwards. To carve, you pull your toes inwards.

If you don't believe you can do it, ski some parallel swings with the uphill ski and make skating steps inbetween. With every second or third skating step you will make a scissors swing. Skating steps are explained on page 77.

Link the scissors swings closer together. As you ski faster the scissors becomes narrower. Vary the rhythm and you'll notice that you are increasingly weighting the inside ski to assist in steering.

The more you weight the inside ski, the less you consciously push it out into the scissors position and the more the downhill ski skids into the scissors because it is not weighted so much. Especially on smoother slopes and when swinging near to the fall-line, you imperceptibly make the transition to the scissors swing opening the downhill ski, which is described overleaf.

Go straight back to opening the uphill ski when you encounter ice or steep slopes, otherwise the downhill ski will slip away and you'll be left hanging on your uphill ski. Skiing around slalom gates will help you to adapt the pace to the start of the swing. Ski as upright as possible into each gate to make the curve as smooth as you can. The wider the scissors, the more obvious is the thrust-off and upward movement.

When the lateral positioning of the gates is altered, you need to change the type of swing. Opening uphill and downhill, alternate according to the situation. If you ski short swings near the fall-line, you will ski parallel again, almost wedel.

THE THRUST-OFF

Edge the downhill ski well to give a strong thrust-off. You need a good hold, since the assistance of the speed in turning is limited because you are in fact swinging away from the fall-line. Thrust off diagonally forwards so that your weight moves over the outside ski, weight in the middle, and turn it gently. When steering, you'll weight it more towards the tail.

Practise transitions from one swing to another. Start at low speed with the uphill stem, then increase the speed and swing parallel with the uphill ski and finally make the scissors swing by opening the uphill ski. These swings all belong to the same family and your speed will decide which one you pick each time. Stem, parallel and scissors swings merge together easily and almost adapt themselves to the speed and circumstances. You may prefer one type of swing or another, but learn them all so that you can cope with any situation.

TECHNIQUE

Steer to the end of a swing. Edge the outside ski and thrust off from it pushing the uphill ski into the scissors position. Plant the inside stick to initiate the turning of this new outside ski, and bring the inside ski parallel. Bank body downhill. Steer to the end of the swing on the inside edges of the skis

REAR VIEW

Thrust off from the edged downhill ski and initiate swinging of outside ski. Turn the hips outwards and the outside knee inwards to help edging. If you turn too sharply you will have to put the weight on the inside ski in order to retain a grip

SCISSORS SWING, OPENING THE DOWNHILL SKI

This should be nothing new to you. You have often weighted the inside ski as well when steering, causing the downhill ski to skid into the scissors position. The tighter the swings, the less you open the uphill ski and the more the downhill ski is pushed into the scissors.

You can no longer thrust off strongly from the outside ski when the inside ski of the scissors is also weighted, so you should unweight the outside ski and lean into the swing. Support yourself on your stick and start turning the outside leg, with a little help from your hips.

Don't grip too tightly with the inside ski, otherwise you'll have to start turning it while it is weighted and the outside ski will provide too little hold for the thrust-off. Neither should you weight the inside ski too soon or too strongly, or you'll need your whole body to turn it. If this happens, you will probably catch an edge and the outside ski will slide away forwards. This will force you into a backward lean, you will again grip too hard with the inside ski – and you are back where you started. In

such circumstances, one error gives rise to others.

Practise the downhill scissors at first on a smooth slope with snow which provides a good grip. Experiment with the rhythm; changing it will make you more adaptable and will economize on movement. Shorten the scissors swing to a scissors wedeln and sense the playful rhythm. Always revert, however, to uphill opening whenever the slope and the snow become more difficult or your speed is reduced.

Use all three downhill opening swings – stem, parallel and scissors; they are just as much a family as the uphill opening equivalents.

You will discover that the shorter your swings and the nearer they are to the fall-line, the more you weight both skis and that the more you swing away from the fall-line, the more positively you have to step or jump across. By altering the radius of the swing you also alter the type of swing.

Mix both uphill and downhill opening scissors swings when skiing through gates, which should be well offset at first, then placed closer to the fall-line. The lateral and vertical positioning of the gates will be greater now, as you need time and space for step swinging in a smooth curve. Compete against a friend or against the clock so you don't have time to

TECHNIQUE SEQUENCE

Steer the skis, both weighted.
Unweight the inside ski, then tilt
inwards to initiate the swinging
of the outside ski, planting the
stick to improve balance and
make the start of the swing
easier. Steer the swing carefully
to the end. Avoid backward lean
— it causes the whole body to
turn and makes steering harder

Scissors Swing, Opening the Downhill Ski (continued)

think! You'll then be skiing instinctively.

For more improvement, ski further! You'll find that your movements will suffer at first as you tire, but will soon become more stable.

Don't forget to breathe! Breathe in as you unweight, breathe out as you come under pressure. It is another way of making your swings as rhythmical as possible.

As your speed increases, you'll be forced more often into a backward lean. Always strive to remain balanced over the outside ski and to steer it well.

THE CHALLENGE OF OPEN TERRAIN

Ski across open terrain using both types of scissors swing. Try, despite the varying pressure caused by ridges in the snow (washboard), to steer the outside ski in a smooth curve. This changing pressure demands that you constantly adjust the edging – more pressure, stronger edging and vice-versa.

Try out these movements in a race organized by the ski school which will be held to allow students to test their skills against each other. Giant slaloms are the true test of scissors swings. In scissors swinging though, you spend a lot of time on one leg and this demands strength, which can soon push you to the limit of your ability.

The scissors swing, opening the downhill ski completes your lessons in technique. You are now equipped to enjoy the Alps, the 'playground of Europe'. Your training and lessons with the ski school may end here, but not your responsibilities. You have a duty to yourself and to others to ski safely. So if you want to enjoy yourself and not end up in hospital or before a judge, read more about safety on pages 90-93.

For safety's sake, learn to ski under the professional and expert guidance of a ski teacher. He is there to teach, help and accompany you and often to warn you as well. He will prevent you from blindly copying others and being led astray. He will also show you what you are not allowed to do and point out very real dangers that can lead to tragedy.

Technique is one factor of skiing, awareness of responsibility is another, but far more crucial is the human element. Without people, skiing would be nothing more than theory.

FRONT VIEW

Swing nearer to the fall-line. At higher speeds the inside ski also grips. Pedalling motion provides thrust off to tilt the body into the swing. Good balance is necessary

BACK VIEW

The upper body moves more to the inside of the curve, making thrust-off more difficult.
The greater the weighting on the inside ski, the more positive the lean

SKATING STEP

You will often need to accelerate on the flat. From the scissors position, push off from the inside edge of one ski and then the next, pushing with both sticks behind you. If you push off the same ski each time you will do a skating turn. Again, push with both sticks. Start with short steps, then 'pursue' your teacher with longer gliding steps from a more powerful thrust-off

AND NOW YOU WANT TO SKI

Austria has 400 ski schools and 10,000 ski instructors who are all keen to help you improve your technique and make your holiday as enjoyable as possible

SKI SCHOOL

Ski school is where it all happens. It is the central starting point for all holidaymakers. You will be introduced to skiing, gain confidence in your ability and perfect your technique by way of five ability groups – plus a racing class for those who are really keen.

The ski school wants you to gain proficiency in skiing as soon as possible and to be able to ski any terrain. The movements which you learn, however, must continually be adapted for new situations and snow conditions and be perfected through practice. 'Only a good skier is a safe skier' is one of our slogans. A complete skier can master the moves he learned on the nursery slopes under any circumstances.

At first your ski teacher will make decisions for you; later, he will compel you more and more to decide for yourself. Initially he will select the piste, the speed and the snow to help you learn, but soon you will have to make your own decisions and be responsible for yourself.

If you bring your children – and we hope you do – we will, of course, take care of them. At an early stage the Austrian Ski School turned its attention to teaching children and prepared and fenced off special nursery slopes for children at Mayrhofen, Kitzbühel and Rohrmoos. Children have a wonderful time there, skiing among familiar, brightly coloured cartoon characters and having lots to do. Many of the nursery teachers are mothers themselves who understand the children's needs.

TEACHING AIMS
The aims of ski teaching have changed over the years. Previously, people only wanted to wedel. Nowadays, terrain and deep snow skiing are the favourites. Skiers enjoy the great descents, the imposing scenery of the mountain peaks and, above all, powder snow. Our ski teachers are the best guides for all of these. They know where to find the best snow. They know the safest areas, they know where the lifts are least busy and they also know what descents you are capable of tackling.

They have not merely studied the piste map, they have experienced it.

Your ski teacher performs a variety of roles. He'll explain the problems of piste and cable car construction, and of local tourist traffic. His respect for nature makes him a safe guide. He'll also introduce you to goings on in his village.

If you want to get right away from it all, your ski teacher can take you in a helicopter to the wide open spaces which are so alluring and yet so perilous for the inexperienced. So your instructor is also a guide.

If finances keep you grounded, join the increasing number of people who seek the adventure of ski touring. Our ski teachers will help you escape from the pistes to experience and explore the many excitements of the alpine world. But be careful, and don't overdo things.

If you prefer to stay on level ground, all our schools have cross-country ski teachers who'll provide technical help before leading you out into the beautiful scenery through which the track passes. Don't think of best times and lap records; just make a relaxing journey on your cross-country skis through the snow-clad forest, seeing for yourself the many different facets of the winter landscape and its wildlife.

If you like hard work, your teacher will be able to teach you the fastest cross-country steps on well-maintained tracks. Not quite the fastest perhaps (the controversial Siitonen step), but certainly the elegant diagonal gait or double sticking. After all, we don't need to become world champions!

If you have picked up bad habits in your skiing, our teachers will work with you to get rid of them and to correct your movements, so enabling you to make further progress. If you are prepared to work hard with your teachers, together you'll make skiing fun again.

For those who are ambitious, every ski school organizes races. Take part, not just to win or pit yourself against your friends, but also to put your ability to the test and enjoy one of the social highlights of the week, the prize-giving ceremony.

For those who like things really hot, there are the WISBI races, in which you compare your times with those of the

---

SKI SCHOOL CLASSES

Adult's classes are divided into five groups:

GROUP V

Level: Beginners
Objective: Snowplough
1 Check equipment, basic safety rules
2 Getting used to equipment, standing exercises, walking, gliding (falling, getting up)
3 Walking uphill, over terrain, games
4 Schussing exercises
5 Traversing exercises (steep practice area)
6 Snowplough exercises
7 Snowplough turns
8 Using lifts – easy runs over terrain

GROUP IV

Level: Snowplough
Objective: Stem swinging
1 Repeat snowplough – reduce length of turn – swing rhythmically
2 Side-slip – initiate at first with weight shift, then with down-unweighting
3 Swing to hill, with and without help from terrain
4 Stem swing garlands
5 Swinging from uphill stem, closing after/in/before fall-line; increase speed as necessary
6 Swinging from uphill stem over slight bumps (stick planting)
7 Shorten radius – open both sides
8 Swing from downhill stem over slight bumps
9 Swing from downhill stem – uneven slope
10 Skiing easy terrain – varying stem swings
11 Swinging around poles

GROUP III

Level: Safe swinging from stem
Objective: Parallel swinging
1 Repeat swinging to hill
2 Repeat stem swing, wedel, thrust-off garlands
3 Shorten swinging from downhill stem – change of rhythm
4 Swinging from downhill stem over slight bumps – reduce downhill stem
5 Parallel swinging with lateral weight shift (pedalling)
6 Shorten parallel swinging (pedalling), emphasize bending of inside leg, extension of outside leg
7 Parallel swinging – vary radius
8 Shorten parallel swing – smooth slope – reduce pedalling motion – open wedel
9 Parallel swinging – more sharply away

AT YOUR SERVICE

A good ski school needs leadership and a dedicated team of instructors to teach every level of skill. It's not uncommon to find past world champions, Olympic medallists and World Cup winners managing Austria's ski schools. Featured is Karl Schranz, former world champion, manager of the ski school at St Anton, the largest of the 400 schools in Austria.

world's best skiers. See how you would do against Stenmark, Mahre and Co and try to close the gap. Your 'handicap' shows how far behind the top skiers you are.

If you have a liking for the more artistic movements in skiing, you certainly won't be the only one. We'll gladly provide a teacher who can show you the great variety of movements in ski ballet — and not merely a quick somersault.

All the time you are with us we will guide you safely through your skiing holiday. Every ski teacher is a safety expert. Directly or indirectly, he learns about safety for about a third of his training period. He knows the dangers and has the courage to say 'no' sometimes. Listen to him when he forbids something; he is not doing it merely to assert his authority. Not without reason does almost every ski school cooperate with the avalanche commissions, which decide which descents should be closed on grounds of safety.

The ski school offers a whole host of services. If you have a problem the teachers and director will know what to do. They'll give you information about equipment, pistes, restaurants, bus services and shopping. They'll help you plan your holiday, and will even go with you to the sports shop to make sure that the equipment you buy suits your ability and your pocket. The ski school is open to everyone. Come and see for yourself: your holiday will be spent among friends.

---

from fall-line — stronger pedalling action again

10 Parallel swinging — near fall-line — down unweighting — shorter swings

11 Parallel swinging with down unweighting — longer radius

12 Increase speed (carve) and vary swings

13 Emergency stop

14 Parallel swinging in light deep snow (safety)

15 Parallel swinging through evenly spaced gates

GROUP II

Level: Parallel swinging with pedalling, parallel step swings

Objective: Safe parallel swinging with lateral weight shift and fore/aft weight shift and with two legged thrust-off

1 Repeat parallel swinging with lateral weight shift — parallel step swings (pedalling)

— rhythm changes

2 Repeat parallel swinging with down unweighting — changing rhythm (wedel) — increase speed

3 Parallel swinging over bumps and ridges

4 Repeat garlands

5 Parallel swinging in steeper terrain — with thrust-off

6 Adapt thrust-off to terrain

7 Parallel swinging through gates — regular/ irregular placing

8 Parallel swinging at higher and changing speed — carving

GROUP I

Level: Confident interchanging between stem, parallel and scissors swinging

Objective: Adapting swinging to terrain, speed, snow, slalom gates

Safe change of rhythm and type of swinging

1 Repeat garlands — rapid sequence of long skids and swings

2 Garlands from backward lean

3 Parallel swings turning from hips

4 Scissors swings: long, short

5 Scissors swing — swinging with accentuated inward lean

6 Interplay of parallel swings with down and up unweighting

7 Fast skiing over bumps

8 All types of swing — from backward lean

9 Swinging on inside ski

10 Spin — 360° turn

11 Jumps

12 Slalom against the clock

13 Simple parallel slaloms and giant slalom

14 Skiing in deep and poor snow conditions

15 Very steep terrain — safety

WISBI RACES— HOW FAST AM I?

People are not all the same. We all want to be different, and perhaps be better than the other person at a given skill. All ski schools give you the opportunity at the end of a week's course to test your progress in terms of technique and speed by racing against your fellow students. These are the WISBI races. (WISBI is an acronym derived from the German Wie Schnell Bin Ich? meaning How fast am I?). How do you think you would have fared in last week's World Cup race? Train with your teacher and work hard at making the comparison with top skiers.

STRENUOUS EFFORT

You will have to make a concerted effort to ensure your performance compares well with WISBI races in other resorts and with the times of top skiers. Train hard to improve your gliding and carving, the line you take and your final run-in. Learn how to start properly and, above all, work on your fitness, it makes the biggest difference.

You'll soon sense that you are making progress, your 'handicap' will get smaller — and so will the gap between you and the world's best!

CROSS-COUNTRY RACING

You can compare your performance in cross-country skiing as well, and the WISBI races will be joined by the WISLI races — How fast can I run? Again the comparison is with the fastest in the world, and whether you use the Siitonen step or the diagonal gait, you are hot on the tracks of the champions! Here, too, your teacher becomes your trainer. In cross-country as well, fitness can improve your performance more than technique alone. Don't forget that, even when the winter is a long way off.

THE COMPETITIVE SPIRIT

Most people, especially the young, like to compete, to achieve something. All ski schools therefore end their courses with competitions and awards, the type of competition being adapted to local conditions. The prizegiving ceremony is the final social event of the week. For those who want to compare their performance with those of national champions, there are the WISBI races and the equivalent WISLI races for 'Langlauf' or cross-country skiing. The final race of the week is always a highlight

CHILDREN'S CLASSES

The classes are divided into three groups:

GROUP III

Level: Beginners
Objective: Open pedalling wedel
1 Equipment check
2 Schuss
3 Snowplough
4 Snowplough turn
5 Snowplough wedel
6 Open wedel — with lateral weight shift (pedalling)

GROUP II

Level: Intermediate − Open wedel
Objective: Adaptable parallel swinging
1 Swinging from uphill stem — steep slope, poor snow
2 Parallel swinging — wedel with lateral

weight shift (pedalling), smooth, moderate slope

3 Parallel swinging – reduce pedal action – smooth then varied terrain

4 Parallel swinging – short, and long down-unweighted swings, smooth then varied terrain

5 Emergency stop

6 Parallel swinging with thrust-off – steeper slope

7 Parallel swinging – changing type and rhythm of swinging

8 Deep snow

9 Slalom gates

GROUP I

Category: Confident interchanging between stem, parallel and scissors swinging

Objective: Adapting swinging to terrain,

speed, snow, slalom gates

Safe change of rhythm and type of swinging, 'fun' of movement

1 Repeat garlands – rapid sequence of long skids and swings

2 Garlands from backward lean

3 Parallel swings turning from hips

4 Scissors swings: long, short

5 Scissors swing – swinging with accentuated inward lean

6 Interplay of parallel swings with down and up unweighting

7 Fast skiing over bumps

8 All types of swing – from backward lean

9 Swinging on inside ski

10 Spin – 360° turn

11 Jumps

12 Slalom against the clock

13 Simple parallel slaloms and giant slalom

14 Skiing in deep and poor snow conditions

15 Very steep terrain – safety

NOTE: The division of these exercises into groups necessitates their continuous adaptation to:

(a) The students. Talented and fit youngsters and schoolchildren with short skis are designated here as 'young students'. They can ski with shorter swings, exploit the rhythm and use the sticks better and work more directly towards the objectives. Older, less confident and less fit students and those with poor equipment have to make longer swings and require longer slipping or traversing phases between swings, need more practice of each type of swing and cannot exploit the rhythm so well.

(b) Teaching aims: safe skiing, recreational, racing and acrobatic skiing.

(c) Equipment: Normal, short or cross-country skis.

TEACHING CHILDREN TO SKI

During the 1960s parents began to take their children skiing with them, so that they could learn early on. Why not entrust your children to the expert and patient care of our ski teachers? They have a lot of experience in teaching children and will prevent bad skiing habits from forming.

Children learn through play in a carefree, uninhibited way. They should be taught in situations which demand the sort of movements required of them.

A basic distinction can be made between the ski kindergarten and the children's ski school. In the kindergarten, children are looked after, kept occupied and occasionally stood on skis. The children's ski school is where the 'baby-run' and the 'ski garden' are found.

In the baby-run the children learn to glide, slip, balance, turn and steer, but without these words ever being mentioned. Instructions are given by pictures or by very general movements with such remarks as 'make yourself as big as an eagle' or 'as small as a dwarf', 'reach out sideways' etc. These movements teach the children how to balance.

The ski garden is an area where all the types of terrain found in everyday skiing are brought together. They comprise, in the main, the 'washboard', the 'organ pipes' and the bob run.

On the 'washboard' the ski tips flap up and down as in a mogul field. The child learns to balance by leaning forwards and backwards and not to take off but to absorb the bumps. Over the 'organ pipes' the child balances with each leg in turn the faster he goes.

In the bob run the children discover how big a part external forces play in turning. They are pushed by both sides of the run and make snowplough turns. They then steer the skis on their edges as is necessary later on uneven slopes.

Every child wants to be a racer and the slalom is always a great favourite. The slalom poles make instruction unnecessary. As well as encouraging the competitive spirit, they make concentration vital which in turn makes for economical and purposeful movement.

Children are adventurous and want to do well. The less able children are inspired to improve by the better ones.

What child doesn't enjoy jumping? He will start with jumps off bumps, leading up to larger jumping hills, always with sufficient run-out and always free of obstructions. The best

practice is to ski for long periods without sticks, which is perfectly safe and aids balance.

To start with, the children ski on specially roped-off pistes but it is not long before the teacher takes them onto the 'normal' piste. He draws their attention to the possible hazards and to the need for them to learn to look after themselves. In the ski garden, their speed is predetermined by the slope, but on the open slopes the children have to learn to control their own speed by varying the radius of their turns and the sideways positioning of their skis.

At first the teacher has to compel them to ski slowly so that

they can turn more precisely; then, cautiously, he encourages them to ski faster so that they start to carve their turns.

The ski teacher speaks to the children in simple terms, the amount of praise always outweighing the criticism. He knows the value of frequent breaks for play and relaxation, since children can't work and concentrate for long periods at a time. The teacher therefore has a difficult and changing role to perform — encouraging here, restraining there, giving praise and gently admonishing.

From the well-protected nursery slopes, the children make their way onto the pistes where young and old, skilled and unskilled, are skiing. Children will always act like children; they will be eager and perhaps 'cheeky'. It is the ski teacher's job to point out how an adult or child 'over there' is skiing at a reckless speed, or how some show-off is skiing too close to other people. He has to tell the children what to do if they lose the rest of the group. All in all though, teaching children is a pleasure, albeit a demanding one.

In Austria, 50 per cent of all those learning to ski are children. You can always be sure that your child is in the safe hands of experienced teachers who really care. Your child will thank you for it. Don't be surprised if a photo of the ski teacher appears on your child's bedside table after the holiday!

JUNIOR SKI SCHOOL

Toni Sailer, triple gold medal winner in the 1956 Winter Olympics, is manager of the Junior Ski School at Kitzbühel. A good children's ski teacher must have dedication, patience and a sense of fun. Toni has all these — and a talent to inspire

CHILDREN'S RACES

If your child would like to race we have teachers who have passed the trainers' examination and bring practical experience from the world of racing.

Prepare your child for training, which has to be built up slowly over two or three years. The child should learn all types of swing and build upon this instruction by practising at higher speeds.

The speed must be increased very slowly at a rate that suits the child. If mistakes are made in 7 out of 10 swings, the speed is too great; if only 1 or 2 out of 10 go wrong the speed can be increased again.

If too much is asked of the child, he will instinctively tense up, lean back and into the swing and push the outside ski away. He will turn his whole body, steer badly and overdo the stem or scissors stance.

Racing means being adaptable and being able to change speed, radius and type of swing to the particular situation. The child must learn how to brake, but also how to accelerate out of the swing. He must be able to switch from short to long swings and back to short again in order to ski difficult sections of a slalom. The further he skis away from the fall-line, the more his weight is shifted from side to side; the nearer he stays to the fall-line, the more he swings on both skis. The ability to change the type of swing — gradually at first, then from one swing to the next — is the basis of all safe skiing. The child should gain experience in good conditions to start with, then on uneven slopes and on ice.

If the child does not gain the ability to change swings confidently, he will have problems later with the slalom gates. The trainer will never set an adult course straightaway. All gates, from the simplest to the most complicated, should be skied competitively against the clock or against an opponent.

If too long is spent skiing through gates, nervous tension sets in and technique crumbles. For this reason there should be frequent, relaxed 'free skiing' periods.

Competitive skiing causes nervous stress. Tension before the race and either excitement or disappointment afterwards give rise to nerves, especially for youngsters. Part of the trainer's job is to help young skiers overcome disappointments, in races against the clock or an opponent.

GIANT SLALOM

Giant slalom is really *the* discipline for children and ideally suits their ability, since they cannot always initiate the swing at precisely the right point in the normal slalom.

The preparation for giant slalom involves skiing the terrain, swinging through hollows and over humps, short and long, braking and accelerating — i.e. skiing 'with the lie of the land'.

Speed should be increased, as steering is at the heart of giant slalom. Anyone who cannot steer their skis on their edges will slip sideways, so 'free skiing' practice with good steering is important.

The key rule for both parents and trainers is patience, patience and more patience — especially while the child is growing rapidly, when the ratios of leverage, strength and weight no longer correspond. If things start to go wrong, speed should be reduced and easier runs should be selected so that one mistake does not lead to others.

MINI-CHAMPIONS IN TRAINING

Racing is the dream of many children. If swinging is frequently practised through slalom gates, the transition from lessons to training is easily made.

Progressively stepping up the speed guides the child safely from skidding to carving. Initially the gates should be placed evenly, only later should irregular spacings be used in order to encourage changes of rhythm

AVALANCHE!

Most people have no idea of the awesome power of an avalanche and can easily become careless. Closed runs and warning signs must always be observed, as the dividing line between protected and unprotected skiing areas is of critical importance

SAFETY CHECKLIST

1 Take notice of avalanche reports
2 Don't embark on ski tours without alpine experience
3 Be alert to weather conditions, such as substantial, continuous snowfalls, snowfall with a strong wind, and sharp rises in temperature when snow cover is deep
4 Take note of the terrain. Leeward and sheltered slopes are especially dangerous
5 Take note of long periods of cold, clear weather and the build-up of floating snow layers
6 Observe piste closures and warning signs at all times

SAFETY ON SKIS

The millions of people who ski each year can put not only themselves at risk, but others too. Ski safety is vitally important, but it is more a question of attitude than of skiing technique.

Insurance cover does not lessen the risks. The 'fully comprehensive' mentality creates reckless not careful skiers.

People today often believe that with good technology on their side, they can conquer all. In skiing, extreme forces act upon our bodies, which means that as we approach our speed limit, there is little leeway for balance and safety.

The skier in the picture on the left believes he is skiing safely, but he is putting both himself and others at risk. Here we come up against a basic safety problem, for only between 7 and 15 per cent of winter skiing visitors attend a ski school.

The great majority of skiers teach themselves to ski — by way of defensive reactions, awkward posture and wrong movements. Skiing like this, they may be safe up to 15 km/h but are certainly not at 50 km/h or more. They lean back on their skis, can't escape from the fall-line or stop suddenly and, most importantly, can't react quickly enough.

TEACHING METHODS
Our teachers always seek to reinforce what has been learned on easy slopes with good snow by giving further instruction on steep slopes, icy surfaces and bumpy pistes, since only an adaptable skier is a safe one.

At the start you simply follow your teacher, who determines the speed and path you take. Soon, however, he will force you to make your own decisions — but not, of course, on overcrowded pistes or when you are tired — in order to help you become a self-sufficient skier.

SKIING SAFETY

The edges of the piste are marked with green and orange ball markers. The green side faces the piste, where it is safe to ski; on the orange side you ski at your own risk. See diagram (right) and photo (below)

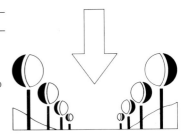

A good teacher will help you learn to gauge how seriously your movements are restricted by poor visibility, fatigue, busy pistes and poor snow conditions. You will get to understand your reactions during lessons and learn to master them when skiing alone.

Careful and considerate skiers observe all the rules of skiing. The most important of these are the FIS Piste Regulations which, if followed consistently, will keep you from endangering yourself and others.

Your teacher will always obey every piste sign, not because he does not dare ski where it is forbidden, but because he must be an example to others. He will explain to you how ski runs are classified, and that you can rely on all precautionary measures and warnings on the piste, but that you are not catered for so well on ski routes; off the piste you are very much 'on your own'.

Only the skier who has learned to take note of the changing weather and snow conditions is a safe skier. There can be a tremendous difference between descents in the morning and late afternoon, especially later in the season. Always ski according to visibility, as you would when driving. Ski more slowly on busy pistes or when you are tired, as your attitude to speed tends to become blinkered after skiing at your limit. Don't be tempted by freshly prepared, carpet-like pistes: they will lead you to believe you have abilities which you may not possess in an emergency.

Above all, take notice of avalanche warnings. The people who put up signs to close pistes are experts who do so for good reasons. They know the wisdom of caution.

The skilift companies spend a lot of time preparing the pistes, sometimes working at night. If a piste machine is operating, keep well clear or choose another run. It is dangerous and irresponsible to follow or obstruct a machine.

When learning to swing to the hill, we practised the emergency stop. Keep practising this again and again, for you never know when you may need it. One final request and warning: skiers have an obligation to help others. Failing to stop at an accident is an offence, even if you are not to blame for what has happened.

SKIERS' COURTESY CODE OF THE FIS (INTERNATIONAL SKI FEDERATION)

1 Consideration for others. All skiers must behave in a way that will not endanger or injure others
2 Control of speed and manner of skiing. Every skier must adapt his speed and method of skiing to the terrain and prevailing weather conditions
3 Choice of course. The skier must select his course in such a way that he does not endanger those in front of him
4 Overtaking. A skier can overtake either on the right or the left but he must always allow the overtaken skier to have plenty of room for movement
5 Joining or crossing a piste. A skier who wants to join or traverse a piste must first look up and down the piste to make sure he can do so safely. The same applies every time a skier stops
6 Stopping on a piste. A skier must avoid, wherever possible, stopping in narrow sections of a piste or on bends. A skier who falls should make the way clear again as quickly as he can
7 Climbing. When climbing or walking on a piste, always stay at the edge. In poor visibility, leave the piste altogether
8 Obey every sign. All skiers should observe piste markings and warning signs
9 Accidents. In the event of an accident, every skier is obliged to stop and give assistance
10 Identification. Anyone involved in or witnessing an accident must give details of his identity if asked to do so

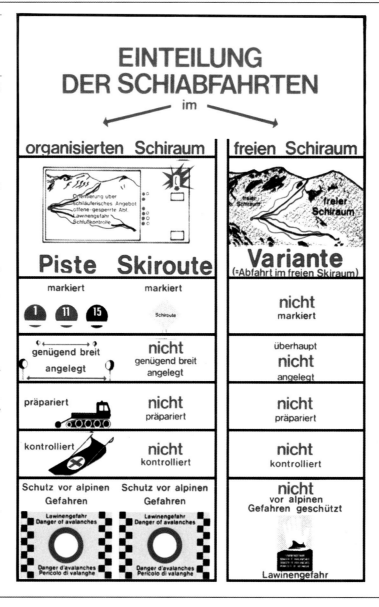

KNOW YOUR MOUNTAIN

The signs indicate the differences in terms of safety between marked pistes and ski routes and unmarked descents in open areas. The left column shows, from top to bottom, that the piste is: marked and graded, sufficiently wide, prepared by piste machines, patrolled by the rescue service and, finally but most importantly, protected by avalanche warnings. From the second column you will see that ski routes are merely marked and protected with avalanche warnings. The third column shows that the open ski area has no such protection and you ski there entirely at your own risk with no warnings of dangers and no guarantee of rescue.

SKI RUN SIGNS

Intermediate

Easy

Difficult

General hazard

Crossing

Caution —
track equipment

Avalanches

Closed

First Aid

LIFT SIGNS

Open bar

Close bar

Open overhead
bar

Close overhead
bar

Lift ski tips

Queue two
abreast

Queue three
abreast

When falling leave
track immediately

No swinging
(=sit still)

Not for
transporting
luggage

Not for
transporting
hang gliders

Keep to the track

ON ENCOUNTERING PISTE MACHINES

Take care and keep your distance. NEVER attempt to hitch a lift. Piste machines operate in hilly terrain where they can suddenly appear in front of skiers. On steeper slopes a machine can slip. Piste machines have right of way over a skier. In narrow sections the skier should wait until the machine has passed. If the skier — perhaps due to a fall — cannot make way, he should signal to the driver

PISTE MAP

For your own safety and
enjoyment always carry a piste
map. The piste map featured
here is of Saalbach-Hinterglemm
in Salzburg province

Gaisstein
2363 m

Schusterkogel
2208 m

Gamsha
2178 m

Hohe Penhab
2112 m

Zwölfer
1984 m

Lindlr

Seekar

34

32   31

33

40

Breitfuß H.

Winklerhof

Ellmaualm 1559 m

Schattberg West
Gipfelhütte   2096 m

F-Hintermayr-Htt.

29   30

Schattberg
2097 m

50

Hintermaisalm

Bergstadl

Grabenhütte

2

Gerstreit

49

38

Schattberg Ost
Restaurant
2020 m

5   4

3

Schattbergkar

Dillingereck

Limberg-
Hochalm

Limberg-
Grundalm

Rammernalm

Staffkogel
2115 m

Saalkogel

Sonnspitze
2062 m

Wildseeloder
2117 m

Kitzbüheler Horn
1996 m

Wilder Kaiser

INNSBRUCK
MÜNCHEN

Spieleckkogel
1998 m

Reichkendlkopf
1942 m

Hochalmspitze
1921 m

44

42

Waleggeralm

Sonnhof

Hochalm

Hasenauer Köpfl
1791 m

Reiterkogel
1819 m

Bürglkopf
1730 m

Spielberghorn
2044 m

Babylift

gau

Fassl

41

43

48

14

46

15

Bernkogel
1740 m

16

Sportalm

47

Pfefferalm

Reiteralm

45

13

Burgeralm

Sonnalm

Spielberghs.

Hinterglemm

Hallenbad
Sauna

Loipe

Bernkogelalm

Kohlmaiskopf
1794 m

Panoramaalm

12

17

11

Maisalm

Hallenbad
Sauna
Tennis

Bäckstätt Stall

7

9

19

18

Asteralm

Bründlkopf
1879 m

Turneralm

Bauers Skialm

8

10

20

Berger
Hochalm

Saalbach

95

POWDER, THE ULTIMATE DREAM

Deep powder snow skiing is a dream experience for millions of skiers but is also a source of danger for those who do not know their way around the mountains. Deep snow skiing must therefore be learned well and performed with the necessary respect for the conditions.

Deep snow skiing became accessible to large numbers of people, and particularly to children, with the appearance of flexible skis, which were easier to turn and to steer. It was also made easier by the high speeds which most people managed to achieve.

Deep snow skiing skills should be built up systematically with the aid of the ski teacher. He will not only select the right snow and gradient, but will also correct your bad habits.

'Practice deep snow' – 10 cm of powder on a hard base – is the key to success on which every type of swing, as well as schussing and traversing, must be practised.

To start, try swinging with an uphill stem in practice deep snow. Use the weight shift more strongly again. Bend lower as you bring the inside ski around so that you can push the snow away with your body weight. Ski faster and the momentum will help you swing. The stem should be narrower and shorter, which will require better balance to close sooner and steer for longer.

Repeat the exercise with the downhill stem in deep snow as well. The expert skier will be able to convert it immediately into a parallel step turn and then reduce the stepping motion until he is weighting both skis.

The pinnacle of achievement in deep snow skiing is the wedeln and parallel swing with down-unweighting. In both of these the upper body remains more or less 'quiet', while the legs bend and straighten as they turn the skis. The deeper the snow and the more rhythmically you want to swing, the more speed you require. On moderate slopes, therefore, ski down the fall-line until you have sufficient speed to swing.

Don't lean backwards deliberately. From the side, a good deep snow skier appears to be sitting back, but in relation to his skis he is in dynamic equilibrium. In a balanced stance, change

Continued on page 100

POWDER PARADISE

Clouds of sparkling powder,
sweeping patterns on a fresh
carpet of snow – this is the stuff
of dreams. But always bear
safety in mind. The thrill of deep
powder is enhanced by skiing to
a rhythm, alone or with others,
restricting your individuality of
movement perhaps, but giving a
free rein to your technique

'PRACTICE DEEP SNOW'

Select 'practice deep snow' on moderate slopes and increase your speed on the piste before venturing into it. Swing from the sitting-back position as well as from the normal stance. Swing smoothly to carve better and make short, rhythmic swings. Always plant stick

STEERING PHASE

Gradually weight the inside ski while steering and let the pressure push the skis forward. At the end of the steering phase, change edges and initiate the new swing with your legs bent. The braking effect of angled skis will force your legs up to your chest. Continue swinging the skis round by turning and extending the legs. Plant the stick with each swing

FALL-LINE

Ski fast and steer smoothly. Start swinging from the fall-line. Bend and extend the legs as you swing. Don't lean back deliberately. Keep the body 'quiet' and develop your rhythm. Powder snow skiing is the ultimate experience.

A GUIDE TO SAFETY IN DEEP SNOW

Fitness and the correct equipment do not guarantee safe and enjoyable skiing. Even a technically perfect skier can bring a day's skiing to a tragic end if he underestimates the dangers of the mountains. The prudent skier teaches himself to be aware of all possible dangers and checks the weather reports and avalanche warnings to plan a safe day's skiing. Even people who know an area well must realize that it is foolish, to plunge into the first descent at full speed.

Slab snow avalanches are the major cause of accidents.
● They occur predominantly on lee slopes.
● They often remain for several weeks at low temperatures.
● Unstable layers of snow form readily in extremely cold conditions.
● The various layers then span a wide range of temperatures, creating conditions for the conversion of the snow into floating layers.

Snow conditions and depth of snow cover can vary from one moment to the next because of
● a change from sunlight to shadow and vice-versa
● varying gradient
● fluctuating wind conditions

It is therefore a simple matter of self-preservation to ski in a controlled manner, where there are no other skiers in sight. Remember, too, that poor visibility caused by fog or driving snow can deceive the ears and the eyes. It can prove fatal to rely exclusively on one's senses and local knowledge.

EMERGENCY SIGNALS

Alpine emergency signals can be given visually or shouted.
● The emergency signal is six shouts or waves at equal intervals of 10 seconds within a minute. Repeat after a one minute pause.
● The answering signal is to signal three times within a minute (i.e. every 20 seconds).

HELICOPTER RESCUE SERVICE

A helicopter requires a landing area of hard-trodden snow 20 m², with no obstructions higher than 15 m within a 100 m radius. Indicate the wind direction by standing with your back to the wind and your arms held out sideways.

Here are some telephone numbers for the helicopter rescue service:

Innsbruck	05222/194
Hohenems	05576/2011
Salzburg	06222/44763
Klagenfurt	04222/43462
Graz	0316/21421
Vienna	0222/830674

HELICOPTER SKIING

This is the ultimate skiing thrill. Always ski with a guide and listen closely to weather reports. Never go if you feel tired. Ski only with others of equal ability. Don't *just* ski, however — enjoy the scenery as well! Have fun 'writing' in the snow with your skis

Deep Snow (continued)

edges and continue to turn your legs as you extend them. You will rock from the easy-turning backward lean to the easy-steering upright position, and this rocking motion will contribute to the rhythmic feel so noticeable in deep snow.

The deep snow skier must learn to be observant. He should notice that the powder is better on the leeward side than on the windward side, where there is often broken frozen snow which is difficult to ski. It is best to ski deep snow with a teacher who knows the weather conditions, the soil, and the snow structure through years of experience. It is extremely important that you observe and respect all signs and warnings.

For deep snow skiing you will need a soft, flexible ski which is not too long, otherwise you will have to ski faster than is advisable at first. If you take it up seriously, you will need to carry special equipment: a rucksack containing a shovel and an avalanche line and, most importantly, a bleeper, which must always be switched on in an emergency and will provide you with the best chance of being found alive.

Flying and skiing combine to create the ultimate thrill. A helicopter can whisk you up to a silent white landscape, opening up vast virgin slopes of deep snow. It is essential that you ski with an experienced guide, who will take care of everything and save you a lot of trouble.

On a prepared piste it does not matter if you make a slight mistake in the weight shift, but in deep snow it must be performed precisely and with feeling. You have to ski as if standing on two feet. If you weight one ski too much, it sinks in too far and the unweighted ski is torn away, causing you to fall.

Deep snow skiing is also exciting when allied to synchronized movement. It is especially enjoyable to ski in time with a friend or your ski teacher, making pleasing patterns in the fresh snow as you go.

Real mastery of skiing will only be achieved by those who can change their rhythm as they please, even in deep snow. The switch from long to short swings and back again is particularly difficult in deep snow because the inside ski repeatedly has to be weighted sensitively during the fore-aft weight shift. It is for this reason that swing variation in deep snow is a common source of error.

OFF-PISTE ENJOYMENT

Skiing the white open spaces is immensely exhilarating, but it is not without its dangers. Accordingly, never ski alone, always obey the warning signs and, most important of all, go with a ski teacher

RED DEVILS IN THE SNOW

The Kitzbühel Red Devils in training. Even ski teachers do not get experience handed to them on a plate. They must train, too, as routine can never replace practice. Virgin slopes are pure delight – even for the most hardened professionals

MOGULS

Throughout the Alps about 22,000 lifts and cable cars convey about a million skiers 1600 m up the mountains every hour. In Austria alone, about 4000 lifts are used a total of 500 million times a year.

These millions of skiers 'process' the Alps. Experts ski nearer the fall-line with short swings, while less able skiers traverse more and restructure the piste by skidding. In this way, skiers prepare their own pistes, and form bumps in the snow called moguls. A large series of bumps is known as a mogul field.

For good skiers with enough strength and balance, moguls are a challenge and great source of enjoyment, but to weaker skiers who have to continually traverse steeper slopes, they are a nightmare.

GOOD AND BAD VIBRATIONS

Moguls have their good and bad points. They make balancing trickier because the ski tips continually flap up and down. But swinging is easier over a mogul because the ski pivots around its centre. The important thing is to approach mogul skiing properly and methodically with the help of a ski instructor.

Start on smaller bumps, skiing over them in a schuss and then skidding sideways. Gradually increase your speed so that the ski tips are forced up more rapidly and you have to push them down again faster.

On bigger moguls try the uphill stem first. Traverse the moguls slowly and when you find one you like, stem the uphill ski out quickly and bring the inside ski round as you turn over the mogul. Traverse again to regain balance and start looking for the next one. Don't be discouraged by the 'cowboys' who shoot past you as if they were riding in a rodeo!

Practise the uphill stem so that you have full control of it for times when poor visibility, a heavy pack and tiredness make swinging difficult. Use it too for getting over large moguls.

As on smoother slopes, you have less time to stem out as you ski faster. So as you gain confidence, thrust off firmly from the downhill ski without further ado and turn the skis parallel over the mogul. The thrust-off is more powerful if the downhill ski is edged well. The pressure created by the rising mogul then results in better grip.

If you swing confidently enough from the downhill stem, swing more often with less traversing. Start by linking the swings over smaller moguls. At first, your skis will shoot forwards on the crest of the mogul. To counteract this, be brave and lean well forward over your skis! Not too far though, otherwise you will not be able to absorb the next mogul and reaction and correction will become a vicious circle – which is no fun at all!

Ski the moguls with a wide stance for greater stability and easier lateral weight transfer. If you have practised the uphill and downhill stem, you'll be turning the skis more frequently in one motion over the moguls. Do parallel step swings and practise them on smooth slopes.

Link the swings more closely together: 'a swing for every mogul'. This puts a strain on your balance. Don't stand too straight on your skis, otherwise you will not be able to extend your legs any more when you reach the top of the bump. On the other hand, don't absorb the mogul in too low a position, or your legs will not be able to bend any more and the mogul will become a ski jump.

The faster you ski, the faster you have to draw up your legs on the rising side of the mogul and extend them again over the crest as quick as a flash. If you are not quick enough, you will lose contact with the snow and lose your balance too.

Ski faster, but swing between the moguls instead of over them. The ski tips no longer flap up and down so much, but the swing must be initiated like lightning, otherwise every mogul becomes a ski jump again.

Don't spend too long practising mogul skiing, however, as it puts a great strain on legs and heart.

The 22,000 lifts throughout the Alps carry as many as a million people an hour. All these skiers 'work' on the snow, flattening it at first and carving bumps on certain gradients. These moguls, as they are called, determine the skiing technique. They will help to unweight the skis, but will severely upset the skier's balance. For this reason the skier keeps his body 'quiet', while the legs bend and stretch as they turn the skis. Mogul skiing puts great strain on the leg muscles, so keep your speed down and don't overdo it

Moguls Continued

Mogul skiing is also hard on the leg muscles. If you don't yet have the necessary strength, the tenseness and fatigue will affect the speed and precision of your actions. Therefore, start by skiing short sections of mogul fields, taking plenty of breathers. Choose moguls that aren't too forbidding and repeat the rhythmic down-unweighted swings on smooth slopes every now and then.

PRACTISE ALL SWINGS

Practise your entire repertoire of swings on the moguls. Not just short swings near the fall-line, but traverses occasionally as well. At some time or other you may need to guide friends who do not ski so well across a mogul field, or you may come across very high moguls with a sharp cut-off. Then you will need to reduce speed and resort to deliberate step swings, downhill and uphill stem swings. Practise every type of swing through the moguls at the appropriate speed and you will be on your way to becoming a complete skier. (You can omit parallel swings with up-unweighting from your mogul repertoire, since the moguls do the unweighting for you.)

You will notice when skiing moguls aggressively, just how hard the leg and stomach muscles have to work. You need a certain amount of strength in your legs to be able to enjoy skiing moguls and you should choose the height of moguls, the speed and frequency of swings to suit your muscular strength.

People often recommend skiing moguls in the backward-lean position, and photographs of good mogul skiers often suggest this is correct. But don't be deceived; the apparent backward lean in mogul skiing occurs when the ski tips tilt downwards, resulting in proper 'jet' positions. Don't consciously copy these extreme 'sitting back' postures. Keep your upper body as steady as possible while your legs compensate as quickly as possible for the up and down movement of your ski tips. In short, no intentional extreme positions — they will come about of their own accord! But if you do not bend and stretch quickly enough at high speed, you will lose contact with the snow and lose your balance as well.

Mogul skiing is, therefore, the fine art of regulating your speed. Ski more slowly occasionally, so that correcting mistakes does not become a habit. Mogul skiing will then be a great source of enjoyment for you.

If you ski with a teacher, you will learn faster and become confident more quickly. He will select the right speed and path to take and will sense when you are reaching your limits. So for mogul skiing as well, a ski teacher is the person best qualified to help you.

LEG ACTION ON MOGULS

The legs work with an up and down motion, not from side to side, and compensate for the up and down movement of the ski tips. Only skiers with sufficient strength can do this fast enough at the pressures involved and still retain contact with the snow. Don't make a conscious effort to sit back, otherwise every bump becomes a ski-jump. Start on pistes with smaller moguls and only tackle the larger ones when you are sure of your balance. It is advisable to ski slowly at first and swing on top of the moguls; later on you can try swinging between them, which requires spot-on timing of the initiation

JUMPING

It's not only children who enjoy jumping; it's fun for adults too. Jumping has to be learned properly, however, as careless and uncontrolled jumping is dangerous.

A ski instructor is the best person to teach you to jump, and he will start by showing you how to jump from the small hills and bumps to be found on any piste. You start by letting the bump push you into the air. Then, as your confidence grows, you start jumping properly by approaching the bump in a slight crouch and thrusting off by straightening your legs. Extra distance is gained by swinging the arms as you take off.

The conscientious teacher gets you to jump from a traverse as well, where the skis are unevenly weighted and thus the thrust-off is uneven. Initially, you will make far more balancing movements in the air with your arms and you will notice on both taking off and landing that the downhill ski has to be edged more strongly in the traverse to prevent it slipping.

As you progress, your teacher will select steeper landing places, which put less strain on the body upon landing, and he will let you jump from small snow cornices down onto the slope. At first you will notice how difficult it is to hold a body position in the air which produces a balanced landing. With increasing skill, you will lean forward over your skis more, whereas if you take off apprehensively, you will jump leaning back and have to fight against sitting back in the air.

Impatient and lively skiers often jump too soon, causing their skis to tilt downwards and ending up face down in the snow. Your teacher will therefore guide you over flat, rising and falling jumps so that you can adapt your take-off exactly to the angle of the jump and of the landing place.

Sometimes you may want to avoid taking off over a bump, but strangely enough you still have to jump. This is 'pre-jumping', thrusting off just before you reach the bump, then drawing your legs up sharply so the skis pass over the crest without touching it and extending your legs again on the other side. This technique is used frequently by downhill racers who want to stay in contact with the snow for extra speed.

JUMPING FROM THE TUCK
Try jumping from the tuck position as well. At first, simply ski over the bumps in a crouch, then try thrusting off from progressively lower positions until you are jumping from the tuck. The different centre of gravity and leg positions in the tuck mean that the risk of twisting on take-off and thus of falling is greater.

Moguls are ideal 'jumping ground'. Daredevils may like to try twisting in the air, making sure the thrust-off is just right for landing on the downhill side of the next mogul. If you land on the rising side of a mogul, the shock will probably send you sprawling.

When jumping, always take care that you don't endanger yourself or others. You put yourself at risk if you don't progress carefully a little at a time and you put others at risk if you jump on busy pistes instead of quiet, out of the way corners.

Have fun by putting some variety into your jumps! Perform a tuck or straddle in the air or twist your skis sideways, but always experiment with care in order to avoid unbalanced landings. Good jumping!

TECHNIQUE

Jumping is fun, but careful training is essential. Approach, take-off and landing areas must be safe. Practise every kind of jump, but watch out for flat landing places. Once you have got the basic form of the jump correct, you can improve on style and distance. You can try virtually anything — tuck, straddle, ski tips up or down, twists — but build up distance and height in easy stages. Let others inspire you, not push you

GIRARDELLI IN ACTION

Marc Girardelli shows how giant slalom should be done. Even at the peak of a skier's career, racing involves continuous effort and training. It is a long road to the top. Structured training demands confidence, willpower and ambition. Injuries and bad patches must be overcome, and too much praise or criticism can obscure the ultimate objective, Techniques change with time, as people do of course, and the racer's task is to adapt to new circumstances and, if possible, anticipate them

111

SLALOM SKIING

At every stage, your teacher has put your technique to the test by setting up slalom gates and you have adapted your swings to those gates. If you want to compete, however, against friends or even in a WISBI race, then practice must become training.

Training is the preparation for competitive performance. Your ski teacher skied slaloms and giant slaloms during his training and may even be an experienced racer, so take the benefit of his advice.

Slalom skiing means taking the shortest line through gates with as little braking as possible. i.e. gliding well and even accelerating. Minimal braking is achieved by edging the skis as little as possible and avoiding the sideways skid. You will glide well on bumpy and ridged terrain by absorbing the bumps with your legs then extending on the other side in a flash and pushing the skis forwards.

Good gliding is pointless, however, unless you take the shortest line through the gates. The good slalom skier is therefore the one who glides best on the shortest line. As a general rule first learn to glide well, then shorten the line. If you shorten the line too soon, you will ski straight towards the poles and your gliding will suffer.

Both the line and gliding are important, but styles differ, one skier taking a better line and another gliding better.

Your ski teacher-cum-trainer will introduce you to slalom systematically. At first he will only let you ski round single poles with regular spacing, so as to give you a feel for what is right and wrong (particularly any jerkiness of movement).

When you can carve more smoothly round the poles, he will set up gates – open gates at first at regular intervals to get you swinging. Don't be surprised if, even on simple runs, he reaches for his stopwatch or arranges two parallel slaloms. Your initially slipshod style will soon become more fluent as you make your swings like a champion.

Irregular lateral and vertical gate placings pose a greater challenge. Your teacher might decide to set up groups of similar gates, one group with a greater lateral offset than another. Offset gates make you 'step over' more clearly, whereas gates in a line make you weight both skis more evenly with less stepping.

Your coach will force you to become more adaptable with more demanding sequences of open, oblique and blind gates. You'll learn to study the course and plan your run, continually increasing your speed as you race against partners and the 'clock, your movements becoming more purposeful and economical.

The elation and disappointment of slalom racing and the concentration required create stresses which affect your performance, so take adequate breaks between runs and don't practice for too long. It is important to have periods of 'free' skiing between runs to relax the muscles which are made tense in the slalom.

Your teacher will use the latest sprung poles. Try out a simple course first, swinging wide round the poles to start with and gradually edging nearer. You will soon learn to suppress instinctive reactions such as closing your eyes, using your arms defensively and sitting back.

Your teacher will also vary the terrain of the slalom runs, helping you to adapt gradually to different conditions. To remain adaptable, you should never spend too long on one slalom run.

Take part in races to check your progress over the week and, if you are more ambitious, enter the WISBI races to compare your performance with top racers.

TECHNIQUE SEQUENCE

Despite the widespread use nowadays of sprung poles, learn to swing round smoothly before trying to reduce the radius of your turn. Try not to allow extremes of pressure to affect your gliding. Don't jump from gate to gate, otherwise you will skid or lean back too far. Slalom is strenuous, and because of this it is a good idea to take frequent breaks for 'free skiing' in which to practise such things as carving and changes of rhythm. When the snow becomes difficult, reduce the gradient if you want to continue practising

113

SLALOM RACERS: COMPARISON

To the layman, the slalom skiing elite all seem to ski the same way, whereas the expert notices considerable differences of style, differences which are mainly due to the character of the skier but also some which have their origins in training. Physical build and characteristics, temperament and psyche all influence the styles of the top skiers.

The characteristics of technique and racing style usually appear when young skiers have finished growing. Premature assessment or condemnation of technique, or 'tuning' technique to that of the current world champion is therefore dangerous; it may block or at least seriously delay a skier's progress to world class. A good trainer should be quick to observe and compare, but slow to judge.

Some skiers may tend to take a shorter line while others glide better. Of course experts should combine both skills, but while a skier is still in the making the innate characteristics of his skiing should be given due consideration. Fitness too affects technique. Without sufficient strength the skier can't steer the skis smoothly or absorb bumps quickly above a certain speed.

Marc Girardelli initiates the swing from a backward lean, emphasized by a slight ridge in the snow. He loses contact with the snow and has to swing the skis in the air with his body turning as well

Girardelli has swung the skis round quickly off the snow, keeping his body 'quiet'. To stop himself being forced off his short line and to correct his backward lean, he has to weight the inside ski in a scissors position. This produces an inward lean but the skis start to brake, bringing his body upright again

Phil Mahre is balanced as he steps out of the last swing. He starts to turn the outside ski with his leg bent. His body is balanced and ready for action

Mahre swings the skis powerfully on the snow and twists his body into a counter-rotation position. He has to put a lot of weight on the inside ski, which affects his mobility

Girardelli now shows how hard he has to turn the skis sideways in a scissors. The outside ski is edged well; the inside ski brakes because of its angle to the direction of travel rather than because of its edging. In this low position Girardelli cannot react so readily

Girardelli lets his skis glide forward into the scissors without raising them very much. While he flattens the outside ski and brings its tip back in, he must keep balance on the end of the inside ski. It is a sign of class to be able to correct a mistake quickly enough to be completely balanced for the next swing

Girardelli has started swinging the outside ski and brought the inside ski round, but the delayed initiation means that centrifugal force pushes him away slightly from the inside pole, lessening the impact. The lower one strikes the pole, with the knee, shin or boot, the harder the blow

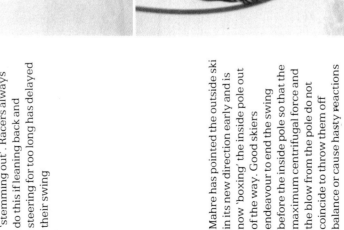

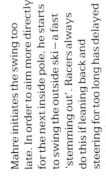

Mahre 'unwinds' and gets ready for weight shift, which is delayed because he has to stay on his inside ski longer than he expected. Planting his stick helps to initiate the turning of the outside ski

Mahre initiates the swing too late. In order to aim more directly for the next inside pole, he starts to swing the outside ski – a fast 'stemming out'. Racers always do this if leaning back and steering for too long has delayed their swing

Mahre has pointed the outside ski in its new direction early and is now 'boxing' the inside pole out of the way. Good skiers endeavour to end the swing before the inside pole so that the maximum centrifugal force and the blow from the pole do not coincide to throw them off balance or cause hasty reactions

GIANT SLALOM

As the name implies, the gates in a giant slalom are set further apart, roughly as far apart as your swings on open terrain. This makes it a natural type of skiing, but at a higher speed.

High speed makes good steering important and this is only possible if you put more pressure on the edged skis by extending your body at the start of the swing.

To steer well you have to guide the skis round in a smooth arc, always putting some weight on the inside ski as well, which should be learned first in free skiing. You will sense this carving particularly strongly in the alternation between long and short rhythmic swings. In the shorter swings, you'll place the skis more sideways and skid, while in the longer swings you'll carve through the snow on the edges.

Giant slalom means skiing with the terrain. Steer the skis as smoothly as possible on structured slopes and your legs will act as shock-absorbers. You have to combine this bending and stretching of the legs with turning and steering; the better you can flex your legs, the smoother your swing will be even on undulating ground. If you become tense or if the springing action dominates your movement, you won't swing smoothly – you'll skid. Vary your speed, sometimes going as fast as you can, but always steer the skis smoothly on the inside edges.

As your confidence grows you'll brake less. When steering, let the skis shoot forward momentarily at, or just after, the moment of greatest pressure. If you overdo this you'll lose contact with the snow and have to turn the skis sharply in the air and edge them hard as you land, thus losing the time you have gained by steering. This 'jet' method is not a racing technique.

Adapt your technique to the gradient. On steep slopes the gates are offset further from the fall-line, so you have to approach them from as high a position as possible. Usually you will open the uphill ski and step uphill to start the swing.

On flatter sections the course stays closer to the fall-line and you have to aim more directly at the gates, taking a shorter line. Less swinging is required and you weight both skis for more of the time. The pressure will force your downhill ski to open into a wider stance and now you begin to understand why, in the technique sections of this book, you have repeatedly made this 'active uphill opening' and the more passive 'downhill opening' into an automatic movement and adapted it again and again to snow, terrain and speed. Your ski teacher has prepared you well for racing.

In giant slalom you are skiing nearer to your speed limit so you need to adopt a wider stance for stability and in order to be better able to compensate for pressures. But don't stand too

wide, otherwise you'll weight one ski or the other too much and the constant weight shifting will lead to a succession of mistakes.

High speeds are nerve-wracking and mistakes and falls can't be ruled out, so never practise too long; make a point of interspersing the sessions with 'free' recreational skiing. Ski up to your speed limit and if conditions allow – quiet pistes, no fatigue – try increasing it.

CORRECT STANCE

For a long time Marc Girardelli struggled, especially in the slalom, against an excessive backward lean, which caused 'jet' movements, turning in the air and strong holding or sideways skidding. As he corrected his stance, he began to glide better, change edges faster, steer the skis along their entire edge and to ski in a mid-stance, which allowed faster reaction. He also began to weight the inside ski judiciously

TECHNIQUE

Step swinging was first used in giant slaloms. It is smooth, round skiing, approaching the gates from above on steep sections and cutting a line to the inner poles on flatter sections. Up-unweight when swinging so as to put more pressure on the skis in the subsequent down movement to improve steering. Weight evenly to glide better. Carefully weight the inside ski as well

DOWNHILL

It's not the purpose here to make a downhill racer of you. What you marvel at on television is the performance of well-trained athletes using highly-specialized equipment on special, well-prepared pistes.

Nevertheless, haven't you ever yearned to shoot down a slope with a good run-out? If you have ever done so, despite initial apprehension, you will have felt the wind whistling around your ears and the pressure of the air against your body. From apprehension, through achievement, to enjoyment. Did you feel a little pride when you gained on a friend during the schuss or when you looked back on the slope you had conquered? Speed can bring pleasure and satisfaction, so let's train a little together.

AWAY YOU GO
Your ski teacher will find a safe section of a run where you can really let yourself go. Steer the skis well and absorb any bumps as quickly as possible. You will then glide well because the pressure on the skis remains fairly constant.

On flatter sections your ski teacher will show the tuck, or 'egg-position', the most aerodynamic stance on skis to help you gain extra speed. You'll notice immediately that you ski faster in the tuck.

Compared with an upright position, you are 40 per cent faster in the tuck; and with your sticks tight under your arms you gain a further 15 per cent. Of course, you need your arms for balancing, so accustom yourself gradually to a lower

position. Whenever you need extra momentum to ski over the next rise or up to a lift station without having to push on your sticks, this egg-position will help you.

CARVING IN THE TUCK
You can ski curves as well in the tuck position, first with one stick under the arm, then with both. Don't adopt too low a posture at first, as the tuck hinders the springing action of the legs and makes edging more difficult. With your body and arms doing everything to make you more aerodynamic and your legs working to absorb the bumps and carve smooth turns, you're on your way to becoming a real racer.

Whoops! Have you noticed how uncontrolled you are if you take off from bumps in the tuck position? In the tuck, none of the feelings you are used to from the upright stance apply; they must be re-learned. Jump by all means, but from a standing position to start with and only as your skill increases should you take off, fly and land without leaving the tuck position.

WHEN TO CEASE
One very important warning: abandon your 'downhill race' the moment you are no longer alone on the piste. Ski normally wherever a mistake could lead to a collsion. A true expert will ski fast only where conditions permit, and slowly and carefully where they do not.

To really see how World Cup racers do it, the Hahnenkamm Run each year at Kitzbühel is always one of the great highlights of the World Cup season.

WIND RESISTANCE

Friction and wind resistance have a braking effect on the downhill skier. At lower speeds friction dominates, while at higher speeds wind resistance is much more important. Not so much the frontal area, but more the profile of the skier determines the drag coefficient. The figures show the resistance at a wind speed of 100 km/h. The disc, ball and bullet all have the same diameter but their wind resistance differs by the ratios 11:5:1. Concave surfaces act as air dams; convex surfaces cut through the air. The tuck or 'egg' position takes this into account

1

5

11

16·8 Kp

0·8 Kp

TWISTING THE BODY

Every one is built differently and moves accordingly. In addition, people weight their skis unevenly in the traverse and when swinging, causing the body to twist and so increasing the wind resistance

2·8÷11·6 Kp

ABSORBING THE SHOCKS

The higher the speed and the bumpier the piste, the more difficult it becomes to absorb shocks in the tuck position. Especially on bends, uneven lateral forces act upon the legs and often all the springing must be done by the outside leg. The skier then stands more upright so he can absorb the pressure more easily. The skier also stands so he can balance with his arms. If he lifts the inside arm, he puts more weight on the outside ski and vice-versa. This is a useful way for the trainer to assess the skier's leg-work and weighting

THE HAHNENKAMM RUN

The Hahnenkamm Run at Kitzbühel is a course which combines high speed with technical difficulties. Every year spectators thrill to the acrobatic performances of the world's top skiers in the race, which takes place in the middle of January when the competitors are in good form. In World Championship or Olympic years, additional qualification runs increase the excitement

INTERSKI

Every four years Interski brings the skiing experts of the world together to exchange ideas, compare notes and get to know the new skiing centres and nations.

There have been 12 Interski Congresses so far:

Zürs	1951	Bad Gastein	1965
Davos	1953	Aspen	1968
Val d'Isère	1955	Garmisch	1971
Storlien	1957	Vysoké Tatry	1975
Zakopane	1959	Zao	1979
Monte Bondone	1962	Sexten	1983

In the early days it was simply a meeting of old skiing friends, but as skiing became an industry and a sport for millions of people worldwide, competiton between resorts became fiercer.

Until 1955 in Val d'Isère, the main debate was between the rival virtues of 'counter rotation' and 'leg action'; thereafter the pendulum swung towards leg action, but a changing, more refined technique. The parallel swing remained the aim for 'elegant skiing' and was confronted by 'functional' skiing, step swinging. Since then, both have been accepted as elegant and functional. After the congress at Vysoké Tatry in 1975 the common features of all swings were increasingly stressed. Adaptability is now the objective.

IMPETUS FOR CHANGE

Advances in equipment technology and earlier learning have strongly influenced teaching methods. Shorter skis, ski kindergartens, prepared pistes, moguls and greater numbers of lifts have cut the learning time and raised average speeds.

The direction of teaching and the methodology have also changed. Initially, a way of teaching was offered that consisted of many preliminary and intermediate exercises. Then, as the standard of piste preparation improved, and shorter skis were introduced, the way was cleared for faster, more skilled teaching. Finally the focus shifted from exercises to actual situations. Learning through exercises became learning through adapting technique to the situations encountered when skiing.

Terrain and deep snow skiing, in 1955 the domain of the expert, became enormously popular and today have a huge following. They are types of skiing which give great enjoyment yet hold real dangers, which is why safety is a major topic at every congress. Equipment manufacturers, technicians, children's ski teachers and psychologists are all working to achieve greater safety in skiing.

During the life of Interski, alpine skiing has spread throughout the world. From central Europe it soon moved north where alpine and Nordic skiing met. Later, it became popular in North America and then in the Eastern Bloc countries. Japan is another area where skiing is making unprecedented progress.

All in all, the Interski Congress is an excellent arrangement which offers the opportunity every four years for work to be compared, ideas to be exchanged, for problems and solutions to be discussed from various points of view and, above all, to meet skiing friends from around the world. The overriding concern is the development of the sport, the ultimate beneficiary being the skiing public.

The photograph above shows the Austrian Ski Demo Team at the 1955 Interski Congress, Val d'Isère. Our author holds the 'Autriche' sign.

FREESTYLE

Ever since the days of Zdarsky, Hoschek and Schneider, people have enjoyed the playful aspects of skiing. As soon as they have gained some control over the 'normal' movements, people like to experiment for fun. Try it for yourself. Your ski teacher will gladly demonstrate some tricks. Not a triple somersault perhaps, which requires months of training on the water jump and trampoline, but simply some playful movements to bring more variation and fun to your skiing.

You have already learned all sorts of swings: now try them with more weight on the inside ski. You will notice that the inside ski steers better, but that initially it is easier to catch an edge. You will also find that it tests to the full your powers of balance: make one mistake in edging and you'll end up on the floor. With a little more speed, however, skiing and swinging on the inside ski become a delight.

Why shouldn't all the swings and turns you have learned work equally well backwards? A backwards snowplough is quite straightforward. Watch any ski teacher skiing backwards as he teaches the snowplough to beginners. The world seems to turn round and a backward lean becomes a forward one, but after a couple of runs you'll feel quite safe, provided you don't choose too steep a slope.

Learn the 'ski waltz' too. These 360° turns are made particularly easy by short skis with upturned tails. The interplay of forward and backward leans demands great adaptability. You'll find that these turns are much easier when you pivot on top of a bump, and that the sticks are an indispensable aid to balancing — which is why freestyle skiers use such long sticks.

Learn to jump and tuck, straddle or twist in the air, but always proceed with care and in gradual stages. Rapid advances often only lead to unsound technique, which causes accidents.

Linking together all these movements you will soon be able to perform 'ballet skiing', and if you need music you will be able to find it easily in many resorts. Alternatively you can play your own tapes through your earphones, but remember: extreme caution is required if you can't hear other skiers and are skiing by sight alone. Your enjoyment should never put at risk the safety of others.

Try 'hot-dogging' over moguls. You will be 'chased' from one mogul to the next by the extreme forces at work. Absorb the shocks in a sitting-back position, carefully planning your jumps, twists, tucks and straddles over the moguls. As always, make slow and careful progress towards the more difficult jumps.

On the whole, freestyle skiing shows that 'playing with movement' can be fun, and that breaking down the barriers between right and wrong movements can give rise to fascinating possibilities.

KICK OUT SPIN

Mike Nemefvary (right), winner of three World Cups in freestyle demonstrates the 'kick out spin' one of the sequences of his ballet routine.
A freestyler (above left) performs a stylish stretch somersault.

PRACTICE

1. Execute all turns and swings with pronounced weighting of inside ski

2. Ski all turns and swings backwards as well as forwards

3. Ski all turns and swings in an extreme sittingback position

4. Ski moguls at your maximum speed

5. Try 360° turns (short skis)

6. Learn stepping over (short skis)

7. Make jumps from ridges and jumping hills

GLACIER SKIING

The skiing boom of the 1960s meant that many skiers wanted to ski for more of the year in order to keep in condition. As a consequence of this, glacier skiing was born.

The frequently used term 'summer skiing' is incorrect, since most glacier skiing is done in the spring and autumn. In the spring, skiers can 'catch up' if they didn't get sufficient skiing in the winter, while skiing on glaciers in autumn is a welcome opportunity to 'tune up' for the winter.

Glacier skiing became necessary when, in the early 1970s, the racing season started progressively earlier and training had to begin even sooner. The result was that 'normal' skiers followed the racers onto the glaciers to prepare for the winter season. The start of the season was brought forward to December, and this has become the best month for skiing in most high altitude resorts.

After the initial boom, glacier skiing has since found its proper place as a sport, being ideal for combining with such activities as tennis, sailing and the like. The morning is ideal for skiing, with hard then névé (granular snow) pistes to please the skier. Then, as the snow becomes deeper, one can simply move down to the valley and, after a short rest, take part in other leisure activities such as sailing, golf or tennis. Two holidays combined in one.

Many other summer visitors want an effortless ride to the summit so they can take in the panoramic views from the mountain restaurant while enjoying the healthy mountain air. Many people visit glaciers on mini-tours, trudge around in the snow – often for the first time – or try out the mountain paths.

Many such glacier skiing areas are reached via dramatic alpine roads with many hairpin bends, and the exciting drive makes glacier ski resorts a favourite destination for days out.

REFRESHER COURSE

Undoubtedly the most important aspect of glacier skiing is to enable the normal skier to retain the basic skills, his feeling for snow, gliding and swinging throughout the year, and to provide autumn training for the competitive skier. Despite talk of stagnation, many good skiers would never think of doing without glacier skiing.

Glaciers are also very important for the training of ski teachers, trainers and other experts who are too busy in the winter to undertake their own training – which has to be postponed until the spring, or better still, the autumn so that they can start the season fresh from training.

So why not arrange to meet your ski teacher again in spring or autumn, just for a taste of glacier skiing? And if you like it, come again!

YEAR-ROUND SKIING

Skiing all the year round adds a new dimension to the sport. Snow and sun at an altitude of 3000 m mean a fast, deep tan and the feeling of spring snow under the skis – or even fresh powder snow in summer after a cold and cloudy night

AUSTRIA'S GLACIER SKIING AREAS

Kaunertal: open from March to mid-December, 1 double chairlift, 2 T-bar lifts, 1 beginners' lift.

Pitztal: open all year round, 1 funicular railway, 1 double chairlift, 2 T-bar lifts.

Oetztal: open all year round, 2 3-seat chairlifts, 8 T-bar lifts.

Stubaital: open all year round, 3 cable cars, 1 double chairlift, 7 T-bar lifts.

Tuxertal: open all year round, 2 cable cars, 2 double chairlifts, 2 T-bar lifts and, depending on snow conditions, a further 2 T-bar lifts and 1 chairlift.

Kitzsteinhorn: open all year round, 1 funicular railway, 1 cable car, 1 double chairlift, 2 double T-bar lifts, 1 single T-bar lift, 2 beginners' lifts.

Dachstein: open all year round, 1 cable car, 1 double chairlift, 3 T-bar lifts.

SCENIC SKIING

The boom in alpine skiing was followed by the cross-country boom. Training for cross-country is advisable. Cross-country skiing is more enjoyable if you learn a few necessary steps, preferably under the guidance of a ski teacher

CROSS-COUNTRY SKIING

There has been a great upsurge of interest in cross-country skiing in recent years. The annual production of around 800,000 pairs of cross-country skis in Austria alone shows that this is no passing craze.

The greatest swing towards cross-country was brought about by overcrowded pistes. Older people and those who are somewhat apprehensive about alpine skiing constitute the bulk of those who made the move from the downhill run to the cross-country track.

Accordingly, many ski schools also made the move into the valleys to cater for the needs of cross-country skiers. Initially, perhaps, these efforts were overdone in trying to make everyone an Olympic champion. Soon, however, it became apparent that those skiers leaving the pistes were not keen on the competitive aspect of cross-country, but sought the relaxation of country 'strolls' in winter. They wanted to travel through forests thick with snow and enjoy the spectacular winter scenery. Unlike the movements necessary for alpine skiing, walking and running are instinctive human activities, so everyone has experience of cross-country movements from early childhood.

In the ski school it is important not to tackle cross-country too energetically. If the course is very long, the normal progress from walking to running should be slowed down. As the Finns say: 'It isn't the route but the speed which wears you out. Speed is for the best skiers, touring for the masses.' Their advice is well worth following. Weaker cross-country skiers should take their time and not try to clock up the miles as quickly as possible.

Since cross-country skis are not bound as rigidly to the feet as alpine skis, they do not always do what we want them to, so it is essential that you accustom yourself to the longer skis. You also need very good balance both laterally and fore-and-aft, as you are on one leg most of the time when walking and running. Familiarization exercises are therefore very important.

It will also be beneficial if you let one of our ski teachers show you the ropes, as the training they can give you in balancing will ensure that problems don't crop up later on. They will also be happy to advise you on buying equipment, guiding you through the almost impenetrable maze of ski categories and models. Their advice will help match value for money to your requirements. Be sure to call on them early, so that you don't waste a day of your holiday.

CROSS-COUNTRY TRACKS

Every tourist board takes pride in keeping its cross-country tracks in good condition. Please be considerate; don't walk on the tracks without skis, or drop litter. Check whether the Siitonen step is permitted. Ski on level terrain to start with

CROSS-COUNTRY SKIING EQUIPMENT

For both recreational and sporting cross-country skiing, the correct equipment is essential if you are to derive full enjoyment from this activity.

Two basic types of cross-country ski are available:

- Non-waxed ski with ridges, scales or fur inserts in the running surface. It is ideal for recreational use, and is even used by racers at temperatures around 0°C because of waxing problems.
- Waxed ski. Properly waxed, it has superior characteristics for sporting and racing use.

As an indication of correct ski length follow this guide:

- Women: approximate height +20 cm
- Men: approximate height +30 cm
- Standing with your arm raised, the ski should reach your wrist.

The stiffness of the ski determines its climbing and gliding characteristics. Skis which are too stiff make climbing more difficult and those which are too soft do not glide well and quickly lose their wax.

The following test will help you decide whether the skis are suitable.

- Lay the skis together on a hard, flat floor.
- Place a sheet of paper under the middle of the skis.
- Stand on the middle of the skis.
- If the paper can still be moved from side to side (1 mm clearance), the stiffness is correct.

In cross-country, the ski stick is at least as important as the ski. It should reach the armpit, be lightweight, strong and, most important, have an adjustable strap on the grip.

As far as shoes and bindings are concerned, if you like them and they are comfortable, then they are suitable. There is a wide range of very practical equipment available to choose from.

Cross-country clothing must be light, it must 'breathe' and yet offer protection against wind and wet. It must also allow freedom of movement. Socks must be sufficiently long so that they don't slip down or make folds near the shoes. Gloves should be lightweight and soft and have a good elasticated wrist or Velcro fastener.

Items of clothing worn next to the skin should be absorbent. Always remember: several thin layers of clothing are better than one or two thick ones.

SHOES

There are three types of shoe. Recreational shoes are high, warm and usually made of leather. They must also be good for skiing downhill. All-round shoes reach the ankles, are lighter and usually of leather. Racing shoes are lightweight and thin (leather or nylon) and fit the racing bindings.

BINDINGS

They should not hinder ankle movement but should support the ankle when you ski downhill. There are three systems: racing standard 50 m; pointed shoe (fixed by cotter or pin); and the LIN system. The LIN system offers the following advantages: it wears well, provides precise connection of the sole/toe piece, releases at a touch of the stick, and releases sideways in a fall. Take advice from your ski teacher and expert shop staff if necessary

HOLDING THE STICKS

Cross-country sticks are longer than alpine sticks. To test for correct length, hold your arm out and the stick should reach from ground to armpit. The strap should fit so that the fingers can push right back on the stick without losing grip. At the end of the push, the arms and sticks form a straight line

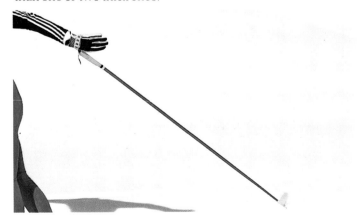

CLOTHING

The clothes you wear must be warm and conduct perspiration away from the skin. Clothing for walking must protect you against cold winds. Underwear is most important. Most suitable are materials which let your sweat through but remain dry themselves. Cotton on the outside conducts moisture away. You should never feel wet. In colder weather, wear several thin layers. Keep your head warm with a cap. Socks should be long and reach over the knee. Gloves should be of soft, light leather with an elasticated wrist or Velcro fastener

DIAGONAL STEP

Practise the walking action at first without sticks to improve coordination of your arm and leg movements.

Flex the knees and lean forward slightly. Begin the step by placing the weight on the forward ski which then begins to glide and thrusting off from the other ski by straightening the leg. This unweighted leg then swings forward, but the knee should not overtake the ankle of the other leg. The arms are swung in opposition to the legs (diagonally) and lend extra momentum to the thrust-off. The arms should swing along the line of the body, with the elbows slightly bent.

SMALL STEPS TO START WITH
Start with small steps and extend your stride as your confidence grows. A track with a slight downhill slope will make things easier. Get your teacher to check that your skis and bindings are correctly fitted. If your skis are not bound properly to your shoes, you will not have the confidence to put your weight on the gliding ski. If you want to achieve a very good posture, restrict your arm movements by clasping your hands behind your back. Practise the diagonal step on the level as well as downhill, but take care on rising ground.

Now we can practise the diagonal step with sticks. The movement is the same, but the thrust-off from the ski is accompanied by a push with the opposite stick.

The stick should be tilted forward slightly as it is planted.

Keep the stick close to the body and push it as far back as possible. The push begins with a bent elbow and a thrust of the hand. At the end of the push the arm is relaxed and swings down and forwards.

Feel the diagonal action of the body as you take short steps. Shift your weight forwards onto the sliding ski without becoming tense.

Practise the diagonal step on the spot, flexing the knees simultaneously and simulating the stick and leg action. Don't lean too far left or right as you step, otherwise the lateral pressure will cause the ski to sink sideways into soft snow.

FOLLOW THE TEACHER'S STEPS
Your teacher will be keen for you to get used to this diagonal step and will make short circuits of a track. Vary your stride as you go and remember to stay relaxed, to thrust off well and, above all, not to be afraid of putting all your weight on the sliding ski. Follow your leader! Copy your teacher's steps like a shadow and he will automatically lead you into the correct technique.

Vary the pace as well, remembering that a stronger thrust-off should not cause you to slip backwards. A little experience will show you how to thrust off forwards correctly. If there are slight undulations in the terrain, you will have to adapt your step anyway. Take shorter steps where the ground rises and longer strides on downhill tracks. As in alpine skiing, variation is the key.

SIDE VIEW
Powerful thrust-off from the toes, using the hips as well. Swing the opposite arm forwards. Take small steps to start with. Keep your gliding leg flexed and at the end of the glide bend it ready for the next push. Gradually extend your steps and walking becomes running, gliding. Good balance is required for this. Train your legs first, then your arms, so ski without sticks occasionally

FRONT VIEW
Steps must not be too long, otherwise you will lean too far sideways and twist your body. This leads to 'ambling', where the left arm and leg swing forward together. If you rock too far to either side you need to restore your balance on each step and the gliding ski is being edged too much. Stiff legs will also cause excessive rocking

WITHOUT STEP

Push and glide! Arms and sticks
swing forward and the sticks are
planted in the snow between ski
tip and binding. Bend forward
and push with your arms until
they are stretched. Breathe out
when bending and in when
standing up. Double-sticking is
specially suited to downhill
sections, good gliding conditions
and undulating terrain

DOUBLE-STICKING

You'll soon notice that you can't exceed a certain speed with
the diagonal step so you'll need to learn the double-sticking
action in order to increase your speed.

While gliding, stand upright. Swing both arms loosely in
front of you, letting the sticks swing forwards past the vertical,
then plant them in the snow, halfway between the ski tip and
binding.

STARTING THE PUSH

The push begins as you plant the sticks. Bend your upper body,
putting your weight on your arms and sticks. Push downwards
with elbows bent and then backwards until your arms are
straight, finally pushing off with hands and fingers. Your arms
continue swinging back until they are in a horizontal line with
your upper body. The moment you stand up again, your arms
are brought forward once more, ready for the next plant.

Here too, it is essential to match your breathing to your
movements. Breathe in as you stand up and breathe out as you
bend forwards. Alternate between the diagonal step and
double-sticking to vary the stresses on the body.

Double-sticking is good for gliding on level ground and
sections of track with a slight fall. On undulating terrain, thrust
off from the top of each ridge to gain speed for the next rise.

Combine the diagonal step and double-sticking. In practice
you'll often interchange these two techniques, particularly in
varied terrain.

You'll notice that for each double stick push, you take one
step. This is called double-sticking with step or kick action.
This extra step relaxes your body, at least on the non-stepping
side.

Initially, kick with the same leg each time. Later on you can
alternate. The situation and track will determine how you ski,
and each variation in speed will introduce you to another
aspect of the sport.

REASON FOR RACING

Your ski teacher will get you to run races on parallel tracks.
This has two advantages: firstly, he can see whether you are
correctly applying what you have learned; secondly, you can
forget all the instructions for a moment and ski instinctively.
Your movements will thus become automatic and stable.

Move in curves to the left and right. You will find you have to
work asymmetrically. With the diagonal step, double-sticking
and mixtures of the two, you are fully prepared for normal
cross-country skiing.

WITH STEP

Combine the leg action of the diagonal step with the arm movements of double-sticking. On standing up and swinging arms forward, push off with one leg from the two-legged glide; first with one leg only, then alternating. As confidence grows, push and step faster

SCHUSS

Above 10 km/h you have to schuss. Crouch down, put your sticks under your arms and put more weight on your heels. A chance to relax and breathe! Watch for sudden changes of gradient, it is easy to fall forwards. Ski upright at first and increase gradients gradually. Bend the knees, step out of the track, and make a step turn in the run-out just as in alpine skiing

SIITONEN STEP

If you ever pushed a scooter in your childhood, you can now apply the same technique to cross-country skiing. Just stand on one ski and push with the other ski at an angle to the side of the track and combine it with a double-stick push. This step was first used by the Finn Siitonen, who found it faster than the other methods.

Don't rely on the Siitonen step though. Firstly, it requires great strength; secondly, it causes destruction of the cross-country tracks; and thirdly, it puts a great strain on the 'gliding leg' and requires maximum balance. It is decidedly a racing step, but if you should feel drawn to racing, then practise the Siitonen step as well.

THE SKATING STEP TURN
Practise the skating step turn too, stepping out at an angle with the inside ski and bringing the outside ski parallel until you can ski as smoothly in a curve as you can in the diagonal step. If you ski in a curve downhill your speed will increase and you'll have to step out less with the inside ski and bring the outside ski around faster. Balancing makes these step turns difficult at first.

You should also learn the skating step, which is in fact no more than a two-sided Siitonen step, and you will need the

climbing steps, the side-step and the herringbone, which are much the same as in alpine skiing.

Climb slight slopes slowly at first. Steeper slopes must be climbed quickly and with small steps to avoid slipping back. The culmination of your cross-country training should be to ski swings and turns like the elegant Telemark, which requires good balance. You can ski a sort of stem swing to slow down or turn.

There is little danger in cross-country skiing, but you should avoid tracks which are iced over or damaged.

Don't underestimate distances, and always remember that no matter where you ski to, you have to get back to where you started from.

Practise without sticks again and again to help coordinate the actions of arms and legs.

Your ski teacher will certainly have advised you to buy skis which don't require waxing. If, however, next year you have sporting intentions, you can buy or hire waxed skis and get advice on waxing from your teacher, who will know the likely snow conditions. With wrongly waxed skis you'll slave away and get nowhere, doing yourself out of a lot of enjoyment.

One final piece of advice: take part in one of the races organized by our ski schools or the WISLI races which will soon be held. We look forward to bumping into you sometime in the winter wonderland.

10 RULES FOR CROSS-COUNTRY

1 Consideration for others. Cross-country skiers should behave in a way that will not endanger or injure others.

2 Signs and directions. Markings and warning signs should be observed.

3 Choice of track. Keep to the right in double or multiple tracks. Groups must ski behind one another on the right.

4 Overtaking. You may overtake on the left or right in an unoccupied track or outside the tracks.

5 Oncorning traffic. If skiers meet from opposite directions both should move right to give way On slopes, the skier coming uphill should give way.

6 Sticks. When passing other skiers, the sticks should be kept close to the body.

7 Proper speed. Every skier must match his speed to his ability, conditions and visibility, especially on slopes. He must keep a safe distance from the skier in front and should fall, if necessary, to prevent a collision.

8 Keeping the track clear. A skier who stops or falls must move out of the tracks as quickly as possible.

9 First aid. In the event of an accident, every skier is obliged to offer assistance.

10 Identification. Anyone involved in or witnessing an accident must provide identification if asked to do so.

SIITONEN STEP TECHNIQUE

This is the fastest and most strenuous step – like pushing a scooter, or a one-sided skating step with double stick plant. The thrust-off from the angled ski is stronger if it 'meets' the body bent forward for the stick plant. Again, start with small steps and work up to longer strides. Alternate 'gliding' legs and the frequency of thrusts. Shorten the steps for curves

SIITONEN STEP IN CURVES

You have already negotiated a curve with the skating step turn. Now leave the inside ski in the track and push with the outside ski. Skiing becomes asymmetrical. First make gentle curves, then sharper ones. Practise both left and right turns. As in alpine skiing, vary the type of step and try out each one in different situations to find which is best. Adaptability is the aim

SEEFELD

Seefeld, the scene of Olympic
and world championship cross-
country races, is one of the cross-
country centres of Austria. Its
easily accessible location, good
hotels, excellent cross-country
tracks and alpine skiing
make it a very popular resort

THE SKI RESORTS OF AUSTRIA

To help you plan your skiing holiday we've included a map of Austria, which will give you an overall impression of the country, and a comprehensive list of Austrian ski resorts. They are grouped by region and feature information about the area, including the number of ski schools, ski kindergartens and other amenities. You'll be able to get the full details from the resort's tourist office, either by phone (numbers are listed) or by post (postal code and the name of the town will suffice for the address). Good skiing!

VORARLBERG

1   Bodensee/Rhine Valley
2   Oberland
3   Brandnertal/Bludenz
4   Montafon
5   Grosswalsertal
6   Bregenzerwald
7   Kleinwalsertal
8   Klosteral

VORARLBERG TIROL

9   Arlberg

14   Lechtal
15   Tannheimer Tal
16   Zwischentoren – Reutte
17   Seefelder-Mieminger Plateau
18   From Inntal to Sellrain
19   Oetztal
20   Wipptal, Side Valleys and Stubaital
21   Innsbruck and Surroundings
22   East of Innsbruch
23   Zillertal
24   Achental – Schwaz and Surroundings
25   From Inntal to Wildschönau and Alpbachtal
26   The Kitzbühel Alps
27   Kufstein and Surroundings
28   Ferienwinkel am Kaiser
29   East Tyrol, north of Lienz
30   Pustertal – Lienz Dolomites

SALZBURGER LAND

Salzburg Province

31   The City of Salzburg, towns in the Surroundings and the Alpine Foothills
32   Tennengau and Salzburg's "Salzkammergut"
33   From Hochkönig to the Tennengebirge
34   Pinzgauer Saalachtal
35   Unterpinzgau, Europa Sport Region, Oberpinzgau
36   Gasteinertal, Grossarltal
37   Radstädter Tauern, Pongau Sun Terrace
38   Lungau

KÄRNTEN

Carinthia

39   National Park Region Goldberge-Mölltal
40   Upper Drautal
41   The Carnic Ski Area
42   The Central Drautal Area
43   Millstätter See
44   Bad Kleinkirchheim
45   Liesertal and Maltatal
46   The Turrach Region, Hochrindl, Simonhöhe
47   The Winter Sports Area around Villach
48   The Region around Wörther See
49   The Rosental Area
50   The Völkermarkt Area
51   The St. Veit an der Glan Area
52   The Lavanttal Area

STEIERMARK

Styria

53   Western Styria
54   Southern Styrian border and wine country, Radkersburg and Leibnitz
55   Fürstenfeld and Feldbach
56   Graz and environs

TIROL

Tyrol

10   Paznauntal
11   Upper Inntal
12   Kaunertal – Landeck and Surroundings
13   Pitztal – Imst and Surroundings

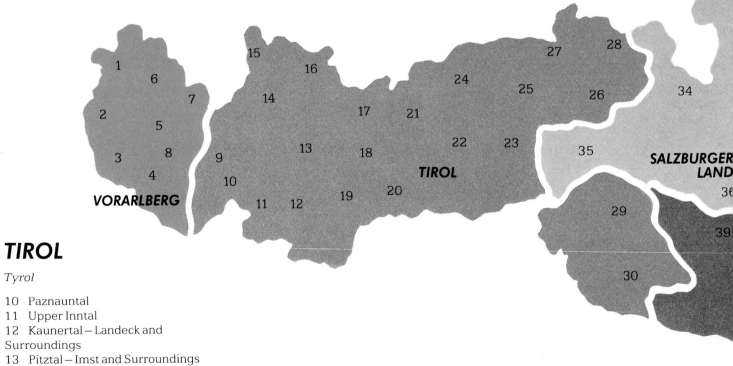

57 Weiz and Hartberg
58 Mürz Valley, Birthplace of Rosegger, the Styrian Semmering, Upper Mürz Valley, Upper Feistritz Valley
59 The Hochschwab Alpine Area
60 Leoben-Präbichl-Erzberg
61 The Gesäuse Alpine Region
62 The Liesingtal Alpine Region
63 Upper Murtal
64 Heimat am Grimming
65 The Dachstein-Tauern Area
66 The Styrian Salzkammergut

OBER ÖSTERREICH

Upper Austria

67 Pyhrn, Eisenwurzen
68 Salzkammergut
69 Innviertel – Hausruckwald
70 Linz – Danube Region
71 Mühlviertel

NIEDERÖSTERREICH

Lower Austria

72 Waldviertel – Weinviertel
73 Wachau – Nibelungengau
74 Alpine Foothills
75 The Alpine Area of Lower Austria
76 Vienna Woods with Vienna and environs

BURGENLAND

77 Neusiedler See
78 Rosalia

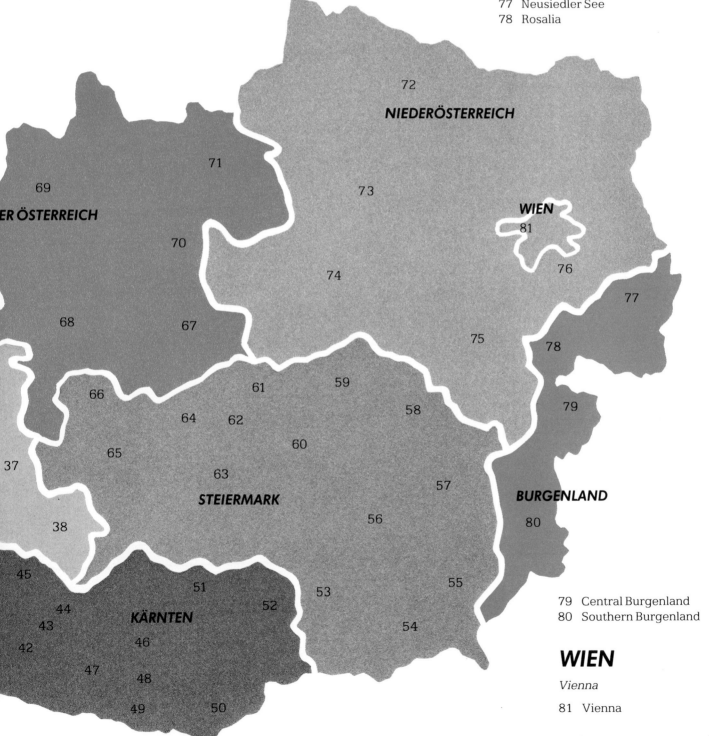

79 Central Burgenland
80 Southern Burgenland

WIEN

Vienna

81 Vienna

139

BODENSEE/RHINE VALLEY   1

The area Bodensee/Rhine Valley with its situation at approx. 1,300 feet above sea level is not a true winter resort area, but thanks to its excellent travel communications with the major ski centres of Vorarlberg, it is an ideal headquarters for winter holidaymakers.

Aside from the smaller ski areas in Bregenz and Dornbirn, a mere hour's trip by private or public transport brings you to the Bregenzerwald, the Montafon valley and the Arlberg Mountain. For those culturally inclined guests, Bregenz offers a vast programme: theatre, concerts, cinemas, exhibitions and even a gambling casino. The area is a shopping headquarters for the whole Province. There is a wide range of restaurants and taverns as well.

A-6900 Bregenz	5574/23391	400 m
A-6922 Buch	5579/8253	725 m
A-6850 Dornbirn	5572/62188	436 m
A-6911 Eichenberg	5574/249594	796 m
A-6845 Hohenems	5576/2301	432 m

SKI SCHOOLS	2
CABLE CAR	1
T-BARS	13
CROSS-COUNTRY SKI RUNS	40 Km
INDOOR SWIMMING POOLS	6
TENNIS HALLS	3
RIDING HALLS	2
HIGHEST MOUNTAIN STATION	1,064 m

OBERLAND   2

The Oberland area of Vorarlberg with its ski centres Hohe Kugel, Laternsertal/Zwischenwasser and Frastanz/Bazora, offers the downhill ski enthusiast as well as the cross-country fan both possibilities for skiing until well into spring. The areas called Hohe Kugel, Hohe Freschen and Laternsertal with its Gerenfalben are good tips for cross-country skiers. For downhill fans there are 10 T-bar lifts in Oberland and 1 double-chairlift, as well as 21 miles of cross-country ski runs. In Laterns there are ice courses where the Europe Cup and World Cup races can be held.

It is worth getting to know this area well, for there have always been reasonably priced inns offering Austrian style hospitality in quiet ski villages and valley towns.

A-6820 Frastanz/Bazora	5522/51500	510 m
A-6830 Laterns	5526/212	900 m
A-6832 Zwischen-		
wasser/Furx	5522/44315	800 m
A-6800 Feldkirch	5522/23467	450 m

SKI SCHOOLS	2
CHAIR LIFTS	1
T-BARS	10
CROSS-COUNTRY SKI RUNS	36 Km
TENNIS HALLS	2
RIDING HALLS	1
HIGHEST MOUNTAIN STATION	1,785 m

BRANDNERTAL/BLUDENZ 3

The winter sports centre Brandnertal-Bludenz offers a wide variety of ski-runs, from the easy and predominantly middle difficulty runs to the impressive FIS-run which incorporates a dozen areas. The whole valley is complete with ski-schools, ski-kindergartens, cross-country runs, foot-paths, bars, discotheques and bowling alleys as well as excellent restaurants and a broad range of accommodation possibilities. The mountain known as the Scesaplana-Massiv with its Brandner Glacier forms the boundary to the valley.

A-6700 Bludenz	5552/2170	588 m
A-6708 Brand	5559/201	1.037 m
A-6700 Bürs	5552/2617	570 m
A-6700 Bürserberg	5552/3317	850 m

SKI SCHOOLS	2
CABLE CARS	1
CHAIR LIFTS	4
T-BARS	8
CROSS-COUNTRY SKI RUNS	28 Km
INDOOR SWIMMING POOLS	8
TENNIS HALLS	2
SKI KINDERGARTENS	2
HIGHEST MOUNTAIN STATION	1,920 m

MONTAFON   4

The Montafon Valley with its sophisticated sports- and holiday resorts has become a mecca for skiers from all over the world. Seventy lifts and cable cars serve 90 miles of superb, prepared slopes. Beginners can enjoy their first successes on numerous gentle slopes as well. Experienced tobogganers will gravitate to the 2-mile long toboggan run. The surrounding mountain peaks are over 9,600 feet high which makes the valley sure to offer snow until springtime. Après-ski attractions include dance-cafés and numerous other entertainment attractions.

A-6787 Gargellen	5557/6303	1.420 m
A-6793 Gaschurn	5558/201	1.000 m
A-6794 Partenen	5558/315	1.050 m
A-6791 St. Gallenkirch	5557/6234	884 m
A-6780 Gortipohl	5557/6711	920 m
A-6780 Schruns	5556/2166	700 m
A-6780 Silbertal	5556/4112	889 m
A-6774 Tschagguns	5556/2457	700 m
A-6773 Vandans	5556/2660	650 m

SKI SCHOOLS	7
CABLE-CARS	10
CHAIR LIFTS	20
T-BARS	40
CROSS-COUNTRY SKI RUNS	40 Km
INDOOR SWIMMING POOLS	24
TENNIS HALLS	2
SKI-KINDERGARTENS	5
HIGHEST MOUNTAIN STATION	2,380 m

GROSSWALSERTAL   5

This beautiful, 15-mile long deep valley stretches through the heart of Vorarlberg. It is of special interest to those in search of unspoiled nature, peace and quiet, true recreation and Austrian style hospitality. Guests will enjoy highly personalised attention. Both the beginner and the experienced skier will find just the slope to suit his requirements. A group of hotels are to be found at an altitude of 4,800 feet.

A-6733 Fontanella/	5554/223	1.145 m
Faschina		
A-6741 Raggal/Marul	5553/228	1.016 m
A-6731 Sonntag	5554/292	900 m

SKI SCHOOLS	4
CABLE CARS	1
CHAIR LIFTS	2
T-BARS	12
CROSS-COUNTRY SKI RUNS	22 Km
INDOOR SWIMMING POOLS	4
HIGHEST MOUNTAIN STATION	2,010 m

BREGENZERWALD   6

This 165-square mile skiing and hiking area stretches from the hilly pre-alpine region to the peaks of the true Alps. It has recently become well equipped for skiers. Wide slopes, from very easy to middle difficulty, make family holidays ideal. There is bound to be snow in Bregenzerwald from mid-December until the end of April. Numerous slopes, cross-country runs, hiking paths and natural ice rinks are part of the programme.

A-6861 Alberschwende	5579/4233	721 m
A-6866 Andelsbuch	5512/2565	640 m
A-6883 Au	5515/2288	800 m
A-6870 Bezau	5514/2295	651 m
A-6874 Bizau	5514/2129	681 m
A-6884 Damüls	5510/253	1.431 m
A-6863 Egg	5512/2426	600 m
A-6952 Hittisau	5513/6354	800 m
A-6881 Mellau	5518/2203	700 m
A-6886 Schoppernau	5515/2495	860 m
A-6888 Schröcken	5519/267	1.260 m
A-6867 Schwarzenberg	5512/2948	700 m
A-6952 Sibratsgfäll	5513/615512	930 m
A-6934 Sulzberg	5516/2130	1.015 m
A-6767 Warth	5583/3515	1.500 m

SKI SCHOOLS	12
CABLE CARS	3
CHAIR LIFTS	13
T-BARS	86
CROSS-COUNTRY SKI RUNS	320 Km
INDOOR SWIMMING POOLS	1
TENNIS HALLS	1
SKI KINDERGARTENS	2
HIGHEST MOUNTAIN STATION	2,050 m

KLEINWALSERTAL   7

The delights of skiing are found here at altitudes of 3,200 and 6,700 feet. The slopes offer ample snow and treeless stretches making them among the most beautiful in Austria. The total absence of through-traffic means that nothing disturbs this country idyll; the valley can be reached only from the Federal Republic of Germany. Both traditional village architecture and modern hotels coexist in perfect harmony.

A-6992 Hirschegg	5517/5114-0	1.124 m
A-6993 Mittelberg	5517/5114-0	1.218 m
A-6991 Riezlern	5517/5114-0	1.088 m

SKI SCHOOLS	7
CABLE CARS	2
CHAIR LIFTS	6
T-BARS	27
CROSS-COUNTRY SKI RUNS	40 Km
INDOOR SWIMMING POOLS	24
TENNIS HALLS	1
SKI KINDERGARTENS	4
HIGHEST MOUNTAIN STATION	2,100 m

KLOSTERTAL 8

Modern tourist centres have sprung up here, nestled between massive Alps which guarantee plenty of snow and offer a marvelous view as well. One of the natural attractions of the area is a waterfall which, in winter, becomes a solid cascade of blue ice. The Arlberg Tunnel at the far end of the valley is a technical miracle and is the second longest tunnel in the world. Skiing areas ascend to 7,680 feet.

A-6751 Braz	5552/8127	706 m
A-6752 Dalaas	5585/244	850 m
A-6754 Klösterle/Langen	5582/777	1.070 m
A-6752 Wald	5585/390	1.050 m

SKI SCHOOLS	1
CHAIR LIFTS	3
T-BARS	6
CROSS-COUNTRY SKI RUNS	25 Km
HIGHEST MOUNTAIN STATION	2,300 m

ARLBERG 9

The famous from all over the world meet here, on the marvellous slopes and snowy runs of the Arlberg. Of course, everyday sportsmen are also very welcome at this ski area at altitudes from 4,000 to 8,900 feet. Hotels are of the very highest international standard and the 600 ski teachers from the world famous Arlberg Ski School train their charges on gentle meadows, snow "autobahns" and steep-runs. There is every sort of entertainment imaginable, including ice skating, tennis, swimming and dancing.

A-6764 Lech	5583/2161-0	1.450 m
A-6580 St. Anton am Arlberg	5446/2269, 5446/2463	1.304 m
A-6580 St. Christoph am Arlberg	5446/2269, 2463	1.802 m
A-6762 Stuben	5582/761	1.409 m
A-6763 Zürs	5583/2245	1.720 m

SKI SCHOOLS	6
CABLE CARS	16
CHAIR LIFTS	25
T-BARS	66
CROSS-COUNTRY SKI RUNS	100 Km
INDOOR SWIMMING POOLS	34
TENNIS HALLS	4
SKI KINDERGARTENS	5
HIGHEST MOUNTAIN STATION	2,811 m

PAZNAUNTAL 10

The dramatically romantic mountain world called Silvretta surrounds this valley and its winter sports areas lying at an altitude of 3,600 feet. The Silvretta ski area can be reached with ease. For cross-country tours, there is an ideal area.

A-6563 Galtür	5443/204	1.584 m
A-6561 Ischgl	5444/5318, 5314	1.400 m
A-6555 Kappl	5445/243 (5243)	1.258 m
A-6551 Pians	5442/4049	852 m
A-6553 See	5441/285 (5285)	1.050 m

SKI SCHOOLS	6
CABLE CARS	3
CHAIR LIFTS	8
T-BARS	34
CROSS-COUNTRY SKI RUNS	53 Km
INDOOR SWIMMING POOLS	5
TENNIS HALLS	1
SKI KINDERGARTENS	2
HIGHEST MOUNTAIN STATION	2,804 m

UPPER INNTAL 11

Old Tyrolean farm villages have been turned into modern winter sports centres here on high mountain plateaus, known for their long lasting, brilliant sunshine. All tourist amenities will be found here: 48 miles of slopes, ski tours up to an altitude of 9,600 feet and a natural ice run with floodlighting are among the attractions.

A-6534 Fiss	5476/6441	1.436 m
A-6531 Ladis	5472/6601	1.200 m
A-6543 Nauders	5473/220	1.365 m
A-6542 Pfunds	5474/5229	970 m
A-6531 Ried im Oberimmtal	5472/6421	880 m
A-6534 Serfaus	5476/6332, 6239	1.427 m
A-6541 Tösens	5477/230, 206	931 m

SKI SCHOOLS	6
CABLE CARS	5
CHAIR LIFTS	7
T-BARS	36
CROSS-COUNTRY SKI RUNS	164 Km
INDOOR SWIMMING POOLS	14
TENNIS HALLS	1
SKI KINDERGARTENS	2
HIGHEST MOUNTAIN STATION	2,700 m

KAUNERTAL – LANDECK 12 AND SURROUNDINGS

Avalanche-free deep snow slopes far from the hustle and bustle of over-crowded areas offer the skier a very special experience. The ski season on Weisseeferner continues with glacier skiing from April till December. Landeck, an important communications point in West Tyrol, straddles the Inn River in a sunny, fog-free part of the valley. The region is noted for its hospitality and its vast array of sports and leisure time activities.

A-6524 Feichten	5475/308	1.273 m
A-6521 Fließ	5449/5224	1.075 m
A-6591 Grins	5442/3827, 3640	1.075 m
A-6491 Imsterberg	5412/4194, 4195	840 m
A-6522 Kauns	5472/6429	1.057 m
A-6500 Landeck	5442/2344	816 m
A-6491 Mils bei Imst	5418/5297	735 m
A-6522 Prutz-Faggen-Fendels	5472/6267	866–1.356m
A-6491 Schönwies	5418/5238	736 m
A-6511 Zams	5442/3395	775 m

SKI SCHOOLS	2
CABLE CARS	1
CHAIR LIFTS	4
T-BARS	18
CROSS-COUNTRY SKI RUNS	90 Km
INDOOR SWIMMING POOLS	5
SKI KINDERGARTENS	1
HIGHEST MOUNTAIN STATION	3,120 m

PITZTAL – IMST AND SURROUNDINGS 13

The accolade "untouched" can truly be applied to this beautiful, peaceful Tyrolean alpine valley. Each one of its picturesque villages is well equipped for winter sports. Icy peaks from 8,000 to 9,600 feet form a magnificent panorama.

A-6471 Arzl-Wald	5412/3300	883 m
A-6425 Haiming	5266/307	700 m
A-6460 Imst	5412/2419	830 m
A-6481 Innerpitztal	5413/8216, 506	1.250–1.734 m
A-6460 Jerzens	5414/300	1.100 m
A-6465 Nassereith	5265/5253	840 m
A-6426 Roppen	5417/5217	711 m
A-6464 Tarrenz	5412/2065	838 m
A-6473 Wenns-Piller	5414/263	950–1.350 m

SKI SCHOOLS	3
CABLE CARS	1
CHAIR LIFTS	5
T-BARS	37
CROSS-COUNTRY SKI RUNS	212 Km
INDOOR SWIMMING POOLS	9
TENNIS HALLS	2
SKI KINDERGARTENS	1
HIGHEST MOUNTAIN STATION	3,214 m

LECHTAL 14

Beautiful little holiday centres with village character, genuine hospitality and guaranteed snowfall. All this as well as prepared slopes, cross-country runs, horse-drawn sleigh rides, well cared for paths and much more. Highly recommended: a visit to the wood carvers' school and the unforgettable experience of feeding game in the wild.

A-6653 Bach	5634/6355	1.060 m
A-6644 Boden-Bschlabs	5635/231, 401	1.357 m
A-6652 Elbigenalp	5634/6270	1.040 m
A-6600 Forchach	5632/25613	910 m
A-6651 Häselgehr	5634/6340	1.003 m
A-6600 Hinterhornbach	5632/315	1.101 m
A-6654 Holzgau	5633/5283	1.103 m
A-6642 Stanzach	5632/268	940 m
A-6655 Steeg	5633/5308	1.122 m
A-6600 Vorderhornbach	5632/301	973 m
A-6671 Weißenbach	5678/5303	887 m

SKI SCHOOLS	2
CHAIR LIFTS	1
T-BARS	30
CROSS-COUNTRY SKI RUNS	124 Km
INDOOR SWIMMING POOLS	2
SKI KINDERGARTENS	1
HIGHEST MOUNTAIN STATION	1,768 m

TANNHEIMER TAL 15

"Really great for winter sports" is the way a German touring magazine described the Tannheimer Tal. This is the site of Austria's only polar dog-drawn sled race and the "Trailclub of Europe" undertakes its training here. Other attractions include a cross-country ski run which stretches through the whole valley, as well as excellent culinary standards.

A-6673 Grän-Haldensee	5675/6285	1.134 m
A-6691 Jungholz	5676/820 (8120)	1.100 m
A-6672 Nesselwängle	5675/6451 (8271)	1.147 m
A-6677 Schattwald	5675/6728	1.111 m
A-6675 Tannheim	5675/6220	1.100 m
A-6677 Zöblen	5675/6648	1.088 m

THE ARLBERG

One of the great traditional areas of Austrian skiing. Famous for the resorts of St. Anton (below), St. Christoph (right), Lech, Zürs and Stuben

SKI SCHOOLS	5
CHAIR-LIFTS	3
T-BARS	26
CROSS-COUNTRY SKI RUNS	50 Km
INDOOR SWIMMING POOLS	6
TENNIS HALLS	3
SKI KINDERGARTENS	4
HIGHEST MOUNTAIN STATION	1,883 m

ZWISCHENTOREN – REUTTE 16

This region has been the birth-place of a great many successful winter sportsmen. The most recent in a long series is world champion Harti Weirather from Wängle. With the Zugspitze massif as a background, there are four ski areas in the vicinity of Ehrwald and Lermoos. Reutte is the main town and is situated between the Lechtal Alps and the Swabian Alpine Foothills.

A-6622 Berwang	5674/8268	1.336 m
A-6633 Biberwier	5673/2922	1.000 m
A-6621 Bichlbach	5674/5354	1.075 m
A-6632 Ehrwald	5673/2395	1.000 m
A-6611 Heiterwang	5674/5103	992 m
A-6600 Höfen	5672/37372	869 m
A-6631 Lähn-Wengle		1.128 m
A-6600 Lechaschau	5672/3388	850 m
A-6631 Lermoos	5673/2401	1.004 m
A-6600 Reutte	5672/2336	854 m
A-6682 Vils	5677/229	828 m
A-6600 Wängle	5672/3601	883 m

SKI SCHOOLS	6
CABLE CARS	4
CHAIR LIFTS	11
T-BARS	45
CROSS-COUNTRY SKI RUNS	214 Km
INDOOR SWIMMING POOLS	7
TENNIS HALLS	2
SKI KINDERGARTENS	3
HIGHEST MOUNTAIN STATION	2,950 m

SEEFELDER-MIEMINGER PLATEAU 17

This plateau has been called the sun-terrace of Tyrol and it is ideal for skiers as well as for fans of deep snow and cross-country skiing. Anyone who wants to test his skills on Olympic slopes will find his chance in Seefeld, site of the Olympic Games in 1964 and 1976. The tourist facilities extend from a room in a farm house to the most luxurious of castle hotels, from a cellar tavern to a gambling casino. There is a full range of activities from the sporty to the truly sophisticated.

A-6105 Leutasch	5214/6207, 6303	1.130 m
A-6414 Mieming	5264/5274, 5685	800 m
A-6100 Mösern	5212/8125 (4125)	1.250 m
A-6416 Obsteig	5264/8106, 8230	1.000 m
A-6103 Reith bei Seefeld	5212/3114	1.130 m
A-6108 Scharnitz	5213/270 (5270)	964 m
A-6100 Seefeld	5212/2313, 2316	1,200 m
A-6410 Telfs	5262/2245	631 m
A-6414 Wildermieming	5264/5336	850 m

SKI SCHOOLS	6
CABLE CARS	3
CHAIR LIFTS	6
T-BARS	28
CROSS-COUNTRY SKI RUNS	371 Km
INDOOR SWIMMING POOLS	41
TENNIS HALLS	3
RIDING HALLS	2
SKI KINDERGARTENS	1
HIGHEST MOUNTAIN STATION	2,064 m

FROM INNTAL TO SELLRAIN 18

This area offers true isolation and relaxing peace and quiet, all within a short distance from the city life of Innsbruck. Winter sports areas have developed from the picturesque Tyrolean farm villages and offer all modern conveniences, without having lost their original charm. Stams is moreover a sport- and school centre. Here, the Austrian ski-jumping "Eagles" are trained and successful ski-racers receive their coaching.

A-6182 Gries im Sellrain	5236/224	1.240 m
A-6401 Hatting	5238/8251 (88251)	617 m
A-6401 Inzing	5238/8121 (88121)	621 m
A-6175 Kematen	5232/2596	610 m
A-6183 Kühtai	5239/222	2.020 m
A-6423 Mötz	5263/6781	654 m
A-6173 Oberperfuß	5232/2794	815 m
A-6421 Rietz	5262/2900	674 m
A-6182 St. Sigmund-Praxmar	5236/209	1.300– 1.700 m
A-6181 Sellrain	5230/244	909 m
A-6424 Silz	5263/6552	650 m
A-6422 Stams	5263/6511	672 m
A-6170 Zirl	5238/2235	620 m

SKI SCHOOLS	3
CHAIR LIFTS	3
T-BARS	19
CROSS-COUNTRY SKI RUNS	132 Km
INDOOR SWIMMING POOLS	6
TENNIS HALLS	1
SKI KINDERGARTENS	1
HIGHEST MOUNTAIN STATION	2,466 m

OETZTAL 19

Oetztal is often called the "Valley of Superlatives". Here is the highest mountain of Tyrol, called Wildspitze, the highest cable car of Austria is found here and Hochgurgl (6,880 feet altitude) is the highest single Austrian winter sports centre.

A-6444 Gries im Oetztal	5253/531103	1.573 m
A-6444 Längenfeld-Huben	5253/5207	1.180 m
A-6441 Niederthai	5255/5400	1.550 m
A-6433 Oetz	5252/6669	820 m
A-6432 Sautens	5252/6511	810 m
A-6441 Umhausen	5255/5209	1.036 m
A-6450 Inneroetztal:		
A-6456 Obergurgl-Hochgurgl	5256/258	1.930– 2.150 m
A-6450 Sölden/Hochsölden	5254/2212	1.377– 2.090 m
A-6458 Vent	5254/8193	1.900 m
A-6450 Zwieselstein	5254/2212	1.472 m

SKI SCHOOLS	12
CABLE CARS	2
CHAIR LIFTS	22
T-BARS	52
CROSS-COUNTRY SKI RUNS	155 Km
INDOOR SWIMMING POOLS	20
SKI KINDERGARTENS	1
HIGHEST MOUNTAIN STATION	3,250 m

WIPPTAL, SIDE VALLEYS AND STUBAITAL 20

Picturesque, medieval villages contrast with the super-modern technical attractions such as the Brenner Motorway and the Stubai Glacier Railway. The latter facilitates an all-year ski-area on the glacier. In the vicinity are plenty of ski-slopes for the less experienced as well. Over 120 miles of runs have been prepared for the cross-country skier.

A-6166 Fulpmes	5225/2235, 2892	960 m
A-6156 Gries a. B.	5274/254	1.200 m
A-6150 Gschnitz	5276/294	1.242 m
A-6143 Matrei a. B.	5273/278 (6278)	993 m
A-6142 Mieders	5225/2530	982 m
A-6143 Navis	5278/296, 201	1.343 m
A-6167 Neustift	5226/2228	1.000 m
A-6156 Obernberg	5274/532	1.400 m
A-6154 St. Jodok-Schmirn	5279/204 (5204)	1.127– 1.350 m
A-6141 Schönberg	5225/2567	1.026 m
A-6150 Steinach a. B.	5272/6270	1.050 m
A-6165 Telfes	5225/2750	1.000 m
A-6152 Trins	5275/337 (5337)	1.214 m

SKI SCHOOLS	9
CABLE CARS	3
CHAIR LIFTS	11
T-BARS	51
CROSS-COUNTRY SKI RUNS	453 Km
INDOOR SWIMMING POOLS	24
TENNIS HALLS	4
SKI KINDERGARTENS	4
HIGHEST MOUNTAIN STATION	3,200 m

INNSBRUCK AND SURROUNDINGS 21

One speaks of the Greater Innsbruck Ski Area and means that the Tyrolean provincial capital is surrounded by numerous mountains with all the ideal conditions for skiing. This is the reason that Innsbruck was chosen as site for the Winter Olympics not once, but twice: in 1964 and again in 1976. No other large town has slopes of all grades of difficulty so close to hand. This facilitates interesting combinations of ski fun and city strolling. And that in a magnificent city with rich cultural treasures.

A-6071 Aldrans	5222/42457	761 m
A-6094 Axams	5234/8178, 7158	878 m
A-6091 Birgitz	5234/8963	858 m
A-6091 Götzens	5234/8259, 7144	866 m
A-6094 Grinzens	5234/7350	930 m
A-6020 Innsbruck-Igls	5222/25715-19	574– 900 m
A-6072 Lans	5222/770063, 77378	864 m
A-6162 Mutters	5222/33744	830 m
A-6161 Natters	5222/21011	800 m
A-6082 Patsch	5222/77332	1.002 m
A-6073 Sistrans	5222/77212	940 m

SKI SCHOOLS	7
CABLE CARS	6
CHAIR LIFTS	7
T-BARS	25
CROSS-COUNTRY SKI RUNS	170 Km
INDOOR SWIMMING POOLS	38
TENNIS HALLS	7
RIDING HALLS	1
SKI KINDERGARTENS	6
HIGHEST MOUNTAIN STATION	2,340 m

EAST OF INNSBRUCK 22

From the gentle medium altitude mountains around Rinn to the high alpine slopes of the Glungetzer, the winter-sports fan can find every possibility here. Innsbruck, twice the city of the Winter Olympics, is just a few minutes away by car. Here you will find an ideal combination of isolated peace and quiet, combined with the nearness of a big city. Hall – a cultural centre with many interesting attractions – has been the site of a mint since 1477.

A-6060 Absam	5223/3190	672 m
A-6060 Ampaß	5222/45464	651 m
A-6121 Baumkirchen	5224/2966	592 m
A-6122 Fritzens	5224/20924	592 m
A-6060 Gnadenwald	5223/2511	900 m
A-6060 Hall in Tirol	5223/6269, 6220	574 m
A-6060 Mils bei Hall	5223/2320	605 m
A-6074 Rinn	5223/8173	920 m
A-6064 Rum	5222/62500, 63235	622 m
A-6060 Tulfes	5223/8324	922 m
A-6111 Volders	5224/2771	557 m
A-6112 Wattens	5224/2904	567 m

SKI SCHOOLS	4
CHAIR LIFTS	1
T-BARS	13
CROSS-COUNTRY SKI RUNS	93 Km
INDOOR SWIMMING POOLS	4
TENNIS HALLS	2
RIDING HALLS	2
SKI KINDERGARTENS	2
HIGHEST MOUNTAIN STATION	2,180 M

ZILLERTAL 23

Zillertal, with its numerous smaller valleys branching off from it, was considered an El Dorado for skiers long before skiing became the highly popular sport of today. The charm of yesterday has remained, even though the area has become a modern sports centre. Here, the enthusiast will find glacier skiing so that he can enjoy his sport throughout the year.

A-6295 Dornauberg-Ginzling	5286/270 218	1.000 m
A-6292 Finkenberg	5285/2673	840 m
A-6263 Fügen	5288/2262, 2970	550 m
A-6263 Fügenberg	5288/2459, 2253	600 m
A-6281 Gerlos	5284/5244	1.245 m
A-6263 Hart	5288/2309, 2331	666 m
A-6283 Hippach	5282/8130 (3630)	600 m
A-6272 Kaltenbach	5283/2218	558 m
A-6290 Mayrhofen	5285/2305, 2635	630 m
A-6272 Ried	5283/2307	572 m
A-6262 Schlitters	5288/2847	541 m
A-6261 Straß	5244/2144	522 m
A-6272 Stumm-Stummerberg	5283/2229, 2704	554–800 m
A-6293 Tuxertal	5287/207, 374	1.300–1.500 m
A-6271 Uderns	5288/2384	549 m
A-6280 Zell am Ziller	5282/2281	580 m

SKI SCHOOLS	8
CABLE CARS	10
CHAIR LIFTS	24
T-BARS	94
CROSS-COUNTRY SKI RUNS	239 Km
INDOOR SWIMMING POOLS	35
TENNIS HALLS	1
RIDING HALLS	1
SKI KINDERGARTENS	7
HIGHEST MOUNTAIN STATION	3,260 m

ACHENTAL – SCHWAZ 24 AND SURROUNDINGS

The six-mile long expanse of ice at Achensee is a Mecca for curling enthusiasts. Cross-country skiers will have a truly unforgettable experience as they travel along the fjord-like shores of this lake. The silver mining town of Schwaz, dating back to the Middle Ages, is surrounded by areas with guaranteed snowfall. Jenbach is the starting point for romantic trips on the Zillertal Railway and the cog railway to Achensee.

A-6215 Achenkirch	5246/6270	930 m
A-6200 Jenbach	5244/3901	562 m
A-6212 Maurach-Eben	5243/5340, 5355	950 m
A-6232 Münster	5337/3160	540 m
A-6213 Pertisau	5243/5260	950 m
A-6130 Schwaz-Pill	5242/3240	535 m
A-6135 Stans	5242/3579	560 m
A-6215 Steinberg am Rofan	5248/205	1.015 m
A-6134 Vomp	5242/2616	566 m
A-6133 Weerberg	5242/8320	900 m
A-6114 Weer-Kolsaß-Kolsaßberg	5224/8124	555–800 m
A-6200 Wiesing	5244/2510	568 m

SKI SCHOOLS	6
CABLE CARS	1
CHAIR LIFTS	9
T-BARS	49
CROSS-COUNTRY SKI RUNS	215 Km
INDOOR SWIMMING POOLS	20
TENNIS HALLS	3
RIDING HALLS	3
HIGHEST MOUNTAIN STATION	2,026 m

FROM INNTAL TO WILDSCHÖNAU AND ALPBACHTAL 25

The valley Unterinntal is famous for its natural beauty. It is an ancient cultural area as well. It is a centre for glass refining and Brandenberg is famous for its traditional cakes. Alpbach is often host to an international clientele ("European Forum") without having lost its sense of tradition. The skier will find all levels of difficulty in both these valleys.

A-6236 Alpbach	5336/5211	1.000 m
A-6300 Angerberg	5332/6305	660 m
A-6234 Brandenberg	5331/203 (5203)	920 m
A-6250 Breitenbach am Inn	5338/738	550 m
A-6230 Brixlegg	5337/2581	535 m
A-6233 Kramsach	5337/2209, 2710	520 m
A-6250 Kundl	5338/326	520 m
A-6322 Langkampfen	5332/7393 (87393)	500 m
A-6322 Mariastein	5332/726116, 746101	600 m
A-6240 Rattenberg-Radfeld	5337/3321	513 m
A-6235 Reith i. A.	5337/2674, 3319	640 m
A-6311 Wildschönau (Oberau, Niederau, Auffach)	5339/8255, 8216, 8980	828–1.200 m
A-6300 Wörgl	5332/2122	513 m

SKI SCHOOLS	7
CHAIR LIFTS	11
T-BARS	70
CROSS-COUNTRY SKI RUNS	278 Km
INDOOR SWIMMING POOLS	16
TENNIS HALLS	1
RIDING HALLS	1
SKI KINDERGARTENS	5
HIGHEST MOUNTAIN STATION	1,950 m

THE KITZBÜHEL ALPS 26

Kitzbühel and its neighbouring towns are the meeting point for the international ski elite. Magnificent slopes compete for attention with cross-country runs, artificial ice fields, a riding hall and an oxygenized indoor swimming pool.

A-6370 Aurach	5356/4622	800 m
A-6364 Brixen im Thale	5334/8111	800 m
A-6352 Ellmau	5358/2301	812 m
A-6361 Hopfgarten im Brixental	5335/2322	622 m
A-6300 Itter	5335/2670	730 m
A-6373 Jochberg	5355/5229	924 m
A-6361 Kelchsau	5335/8105	800 m
A-6365 Kirchberg	5357/2309, 2688	860 m
A-6370 Kitzbühel	5356/2155 2272	760 m
A-6372 Oberndorf	5352/2927	700 m
A-6370 Reith bei Kitzbühel	5356/5465	800 m
A-6306 Söll	5333/5216	703 m
A-6363 Westendorf	5334/6230,	800 m

SKI SCHOOLS	12
CABLE CARS	5
CHAIR LIFTS	36
T-BARS	81
CROSS-COUNTRY SKI RUNS	242 Km
INDOOR SWIMMING POOLS	26
TENNIS HALLS	3
RIDING HALLS	1
SKI KINDERGARTENS	11
HIGHEST MOUNTAIN STATION	1,995 m

KUFSTEIN AND SURROUNDINGS 27

Guests coming from Germany arrive on Austrian soil here. In the shadow of the mighty mountain "Wilder Kaiser" you will find well cared for cross-country ski runs, stunning slopes and — a speciality of this area — many miles of natural toboggan runs. Ice skating and curling can be enjoyed in Kufstein at any time thanks to artificial ice.

A-6300 Angarth	5332/4326	500 m
A-6323 Bad Häring	5332/7280 (4557)	630 m
A-6341 Ebbs	5373/2326, 2960	473 m
A-6343 Erl	5373/8117	476 m
A-6335 Hinterthiersee	5376/24597 (5597)	866 m
A-6322 Kirchbichl	5332/7151 (87151)	520 m
A-6330 Kufstein	5372/2207	503 m
A-6335 Landl	5376/34190 (5880)	700 m
A-6342 Niederndorf	5373/2557	500 m
A-6351 Scheffau	5358/8137	752 m
A-6330 Schwoich	5372/8190	580 m
A-6335 Thiersee	5376/230 (5230)	760 m

SKI SCHOOLS	3
CHAIR LIFTS	6
T-BARS	41
CROSS-COUNTRY SKI RUNS	237 Km
INDOOR SWIMMING POOLS	6
TENNIS HALLS	2
RIDING HALLS	4
SKI KINDERGARTENS	1
HIGHEST MOUNTAIN STATION	1,676 m

FERIENWINKEL AM KAISER 28

Particularly sunny yet nevertheless with guaranteed snowfall, this 1,900-foot high valley near the Bavarian border offers free ski buses to provide easy access to the lifts. All facilities for tobogganing, cross-country skiing, ice skating and riding are available and 57 miles of hiking paths are kept free of snow.

A-6383 Erpfendorf	5352/8150	631 m
A-6391 Fieberbrunn	5354/6304, 6305	800 m
A-6353 Going	5358/2438	800 m
A-6395 Hochfilzen	5359/363	970 m
A-6382 Kirchdorf	5352/3136	640 m
A-6345 Kössen	5375/6287	600 m
A-6391 St. Jakob i. H.	5354/8159	855 m
A-6380 St. Johann i. T.	5352/2218	660 m
A-6393 St. Ulrich am Pillersee	5354/8192	830 m
A-6345 Schwendt	5375/6816	697 m
A-6384 Waidring	5353/5242	781 m
A-6344 Walchsee	5374/5223	668 m

SKI SCHOOLS	9
CABLE CARS	2
CHAIR LIFTS	17
T-BARS	67
CROSS-COUNTRY SKI RUNS	469 Km
INDOOR SWIMMING POOLS	19
TENNIS HALLS	4
RIDING HALLS	3
SKI KINDERGARTENS	7
HIGHEST MOUNTAIN STATION	1,870 m

EAST TYROL, NORTH OF LIENZ 29

This area is noted for its sure snowfall and its high number of sunny hours per year. The mountain station of Goldried in Matrei offers a panoramic view of more than two dozen 9,600-foot high peaks. It can be reached safely and easily the whole year thanks to the Felbertauern Tunnel. A few miles away from the main road, you will find unspoiled farm houses and very reasonable accommodation.

A-9961 Hopfgarten i. D.	4872/5356	1.104 m
A-9953 Huben	4872/5238	820 m
A-9981 Kals am Großglockner	4876/211	1.325 m
A-9971 Matrei i. O.	4875/6709, 6527	1.000 m
A-9974 Prägraten	4877/217 (5217)	1.312 m
A-9963 St. Jakob i. D.	4873/5228, 5265	1.389 m
A-9962 St. Veit i. D.	4879/336	1.500 m
A-9972 Virgen	4874/5210	1.194 m

SKI SCHOOLS	3
CHAIR LIFTS	6
T-BARS	23
CROSS-COUNTRY SKI RUNS	132 Km
INDOOR SWIMMING POOLS	6
TENNIS HALLS	1
RIDING HALLS	1
SKI KINDERGARTENS	2
HIGHEST MOUNTAIN STATION	2,450 m

PUSTERTAL – LIENZ DOLOMITES 30

More than 200 hours of sun are measured every month in winter here in Pustertal. The cross-country run is especially known for variety: the so-called "Grenzland Run" connects three towns, Kartitsch, Ober- and Untertilliach. The Dolomite city of Lienz is particularly proud of its excellent inter-valley lift connections. The large area called "Zettersfeld" is ideal for skiers and sun worshippers alike.

A-9900 Lienze-Lienzer Dolomiten	4852/4747	720 m
A-9951 Ainet	4853/5290, 5216	750 m
A-9900 Amlach	4852/35044	687 m
A-9991 Dölsach	4852/8140	737 m
A-9991 Iselsberg-Stronach	4852/4117, 4106	1.000– 1.204 m
A-9900 Lavant	4852/8216	675 m
A-9782 Nikolsdorf	4858/227, 308	650 m
A-9900 Oberlienz	4852/4759, 3470	756 m
A-9911 Thal-Assling	4855/444	800– 1.200 m
A-9900 Tristach	4852/2094	670 m

Pusteral:

A-9913 Abfaltersbach	4846/210 (6210)	982 m
A-9913 Anras	4846/205 (6205)	1.260 m
A-9931 Außervillgraten	4843/5333	1.286 m
A-9920 Heinfels	4842/6262	1.100 m
A-9932 Innervillgraten	4843/39494 (5194)	1.402 m
A-9941 Kartitsch	4848/216 (5216)	1.356 m
A-9942 Obertilliach	4847/255 (5255)	1.450 m
A-9920 Sillian	4842/6280	1.100 m
A-9920 Strassen	4846/336 (6336)	1.098 m

SKI SCHOOLS	4
CABLE CARS	1
CHAIR LIFTS	4
T-BARS	27
CROSS-COUNTRY SKI RUNS	218 Km
INDOOR SWIMMING POOLS	6
TENNIS HALLS	2
SKI KINDERGARTENS	2
HIGHEST MOUNTAIN STATION	2,407 m

THE CITY OF SALZBURG, TOWNS IN THE SURROUNDINGS AND THE ALPINE FOOTHILLS 31

Winter has its own attractions in the City of Salzburg, not only for music fans, but also for those who want to have the snow covered Old Town all to themselves and get to know its towers and domes. And should the visitor suddenly feel the need for a little skiing, there is no problem: the most beautiful skiing areas of Salzburg Province are less than an hour away by car. For those guests who are primarily looking for rest and recreation, there are seven small holiday villages near the city. They call themselves the neighbourhood towns of Salzburg and live shoulder to shoulder with the city.

*Stadtverkehrsbüro, Auerspergstraße 7,
A-5024 Salzburg,
Tel. 6222/74620, Telex 633486*

*Arbeitskreis Umgebungsorte der Stadt Salzburg,
A-5081 Anif, Verkehrsverein, Tel. 6246/2365*

SKI SCHOOLS	2
CABLE CARS	1
T-BARS	4
CROSS-COUNTRY SKI RUNS	21 Km
INDOOR SWIMMING POOLS	12
TENNIS HALLS	13
RIDING HALLS	4
HIGHEST MOUNTAIN STATION	1,120 m

THE TYROL

The heartland of Austrian skiing with resorts of great sophistication and simple homely atmosphere. The selection here includes (clockwise) Ischgl, Kitzbühel, Igls, Niederau, Söll

TENNENGAU AND SALZBURG'S "SALZKAMMERGUT" — 32

After a day of skiing in Tennengau, rest and recreation are the order of the day. Beginners feel at home on easy and middle difficulty slopes. The winter sports centres of Salzburg's "Salzkammergut" are especially attractive to those who want to be near the Mozart city of Salzburg. There is Alpine and Nordic skiing at the famous Wolfgang Lake, on Zwölferhorn and on Postalm.

Fremdenverkehrsverband Tennengau,
A-5400 Hallein, Postfach 7,
Tel. 6245/4259, Telex 631042

A-5441 Abtenau	*6243/293*	*712 m*
	(2293)	
A-5524 Annaberg	*6463/8125*	*777 m*
A-5422 Bad Dürrnberg	*6245/5185*	*800 m*
A-5421 Krispl-Gaißau	*6240/211*	*927 m*
A-5431 Kuchl	*6244/6227*	*469 m*
A-5523 Lungötz	*6463/212*	*850 m*
A-5442 Rußbach	*6242/206*	*817 m*
A-5522 St. Martin am	*6463/7288*	*1.000 m*
Tennengebirge		

Arbeitskreis Salzburger Salzkammergut,
A-5340 St. Gilgen,
Tel. 6227/348, Telex 632607

A-5324 Faistenau	*6228/314*	*786 m*
A-5324 Hintersee	*6224/214-3*	*746 m*
A-5340 St. Gilgen	*6227/348*	*546 m*
A-5350 Strobl	*6137/255*	*544 m*

SKI SCHOOLS	10
CABLE CARS	2
CHAIR LIFTS	6
T-BARS	72
CROSS-COUNTRY SKI RUNS	244 Km
INDOOR SWIMMING POOLS	14
TENNIS HALLS	1
RIDING HALLS	4
SKI KINDERGARTENS	1
HIGHEST MOUNTAIN STATION	1,618 m

FROM HOCHKÖNIG TO THE TENNENGEBIRGE — 33

One idyllic ski village after the other thread their way through the region from Mühlbach am Hochkönig to Werfenweng at the foot of the mountain range called Tennengebirge. It's all just a stone's throw from the Tauern Motorway. These villages do not offer "high life" but typically more Austrian style hospitality to their guests. There is a wide range of possibilities for the ski enthusiast: slopes at a height of from 1,600 to 6,000 feet are found here. It's ideal for beginners and experts, singles and families.

Interessengemeinschaft vom Hochkönig zum
Tennengebirge, A-5505 Mühlbach/Hochkönig,
Tel. 6467/235

A-5550 Bischofshofen	*6462/2471*	*547 m*
A-5505 Mühlbach am	*6467/235*	*853 m*
Hochkönig		
A-5452 Pfarrwerfen	*6468/390*	*538 m*
A-5450 Werfen	*6468/388*	*620 m*
A-5453 Werfenweng	*6466/420*	*1.000 m*

SKI SCHOOLS	3
CHAIR LIFTS	5
T-BARS	30
CROSS-COUNTRY SKI RUNS	75 Km
INDOOR SWIMMING POOLS	8
TENNIS HALLS	1
SKI KINDERGARTENS	2
HIGHEST MOUNTAIN STATION	1,883 m

PINZGAUER SAALACHTAL — 34

The Saalachtal in Pinzgau offers a fascinating environment in which mountains — most of them at least 6,400 feet high — provide not only wonderful ski slopes but also broad valleys, ideal for the cross-country skier. A particular magnet in the region is Saalbach-Hinterglemm, known for one of the largest ski areas in Austria with its excellent inter-valley lift connections and sophisticated après-ski attractions.

Gebietsverband Pinzgauer Saalachtal,
A-5760 Saalfelden,
Tel 6582/2458, Telex 66519

A-5771 Leogang	*6583/234*	*800 m*
A-5090 Lofer	*6588/321*	*639 m*
A-5751 Maishofen	*6542/8318*	*764 m*
A-5761 Maria Alm	*6584/316*	*800 m*
A-5753 Saalbach-	*6541/7272*	*1.003 m*
Hinterglemm		
A-5760 Saalfelden	*6582/2513*	*744 m*
A-5091 Unken	*6589/245*	*564 m*

SKI SCHOOLS	13
CABLE CARS	2
CHAIR LIFTS	15
T-BARS	56
CROSS-COUNTRY SKI RUNS	260 Km
INDOOR SWIMMING POOLS	25
TENNIS HALLS	2
RIDING HALLS	1
SKI KINDERGARTENS	5
HIGHEST MOUNTAIN STATION	2,020 m

UNTERPINZGAU, EUROPA SPORT REGION, OBERPINZGAU — 35

The popular ski area around Zell am See and Kaprun borders directly on Oberpinzgau with its thriving holiday towns. There is something for every skier, whether he prefers to snap on his skis in the valley or start right off in an alpine region. The hottest tip for up-to-the-minute skiers is the ski area at the lake of Weiss-See with its superb new 6,700-foot high Alpine Centre. And those that just can't get enough of their favourite sport in winter can also enjoy glacier skiing on the Kitzsteinhorn during the summer months.

Gebietsverband Europa-Sportregion,
A-5700 Zell am See, Kurverwaltung,
Tel 6542/2600, Telex 66617

A-5710 Kaprun	*6547/8644*	*800 m*
A-5700 Zell am See	*6542/2600*	*758 m*

Gebietsverband Oberpinzgau,
A-5730 Mittersill,
Tel. 6562/4519/287, Telex 66657

A-5742 Königsleiten	*6564/8224*	*1.600 m*
A-5743 Krimml	*6564/239*	*1.076 m*
A-5730 Mittersill	*6562/369*	*789 m*
A-5741 Neukirchen am	*6565/256*	*856 m*
Großvenediger		
A-5723 Uttendorf/Weißsee	*6563/279*	*807 m*

Gebietsverband Unterpinzgau, A-5661 Rauris,
Postfach 25, Tel. 6544/666, Telex 66686

A-5671 Bruck a. d.	*6545/295*	*758 m*
Großglocknerstr.		
A-5672 Fusch a.d.	*6546/236*	*805 m*
Großglocknerstr.		
A-5661 Rauris	*6544/237*	*950 m*

SKI SCHOOLS	11
CABLE CARS	6
CHAIR LIFTS	21
T-BARS	60
CROSS-COUNTRY SKI RUNS	214 Km
INDOOR SWIMMING POOLS	43
TENNIS HALLS	5
RIDING HALLS	2
SKI KINDERGARTENS	5
HIGHEST MOUNTAIN STATION	3,029 m

GASTEINERTAL, GROSSARLTAL — 36

Gasteinertal enjoys its international reputation because of its traditional spas and the alpine valley countryside at the foot of Hohe Tauern is among the leading ski areas of the Alps. Five large ski areas with more than 50 cable cars and ski-lifts are available for the visitor as well as a great many other sports attractions such as cross-country skiing, tennis, riding or simply a swim in one of the famous thermal baths. And there is another possibility for a stay in Gasteinertal — a winter holiday can be combined with a health regimen as well. Visitors may care to make a short excursion to nearby Grossarltal. The inter-valley lift connexion Dorfgastein-Grossarl — the first in the province of Salzburg by the way — makes it possible. Or find your accommodation in Grossarl from the beginning and make your excursions to Gasteinertal. Deep in the valley yet another delight is waiting for you: the winter holiday village of Hüttschlag, the very model of a fairy tale setting.

Interessengemeinschaft Gasteinertal,
A-5630 Bad Hofgastein, Kurverwaltung,
Tel. 6432/429-0, Telex 67796

A-5640 Badgastein	*6434/2532-65*	
		1.083 m
A-5630 Bad Hofgastein	*6432/429-0*	*870 m*
A-5632 Dorfgastein	*6433/277*	*835 m*

Interessengemeinschaft Großarltal,
A-5611 Großarl, Tel. 6414/281

A-5611 Großarl	*6414/281*	*920 m*
A-5612 Hüttschlag	*6417/204*	*1.020 m*

SKI SCHOOLS	4
CABLE CARS	4
CHAIR LIFTS	16
T-BARS	44
CROSS-COUNTRY SKI RUNS	122 Km
INDOOR SWIMMING POOLS	31
TENNIS HALLS	3
RIDING HALLS	1
SKI KINDERGARTENS	3
HIGHEST MOUNTAIN STATION	2,680 m

RADSTÄDTER TAUERN, PONGAU SUN TERRACE — 37

Ten winter sport centres with two cable cars and over 130 lifts compose one of the most attractive ski areas in the whole of Salzburg Province. No less than six inter-valley lift connexions invite you to travel with your own skis to the next valley, and all this well into spring. This is above all true of the well-known international ski centre at Obertauern, which, at an altitude of 5,400 feet, is situated in the

SALZBURGERLAND
A superb region with resorts to suit every skiing ability. Featured here are Saalbach-Hinterglemm (left) and Zell am See (right)

STYRIA
Great skiing for beginners to expert. The resort of Schladming is featured (below)

149

very heart of Radstädter Tauern. Numerous hotels and pensions offering every imaginable comfort have long been a feature of the region. The northern equivalent to the ski area of Radstädter Tauern is the so-called Pongau Sun Terrace, a plateau whose name says everything: a net of cross-country runs connect the sun towns of Goldegg, St. Veit and Schwarzach in a delightful area encompassing more than 36 miles.

Interessengemeinschaft Radstädter Tauern, A-5550 Radstadt, Tel. 6452/305, Telex 67744

A-5541 Alternmarkt-Zauchensee	6452/511	850 m
A-5531 Eben im Pongau	6464/8194	855 m
A-5532 Filzmoos	6453/235	1.057 m
A-5542 Flachau	6457/214	925 m
A-5602 Kleinarl	6418/206	1.014 m
A-5562 Obertauern/Untertauern	6456/252	1.740 m
A-5550 Radstadt	6452/7472	856 m
A-5600 St. Johann/Alpendorf	6412/465	650 m
A-5602 Wagrain	6413/265	900 m

Interessengemeinschaft Pongauer Sonnenterrasse, A-5622 Goldegg. Tel. 6415/8131, Telex 67672

| A-5622 Goldegg | 6415/8131 | 825 m |

SKI SCHOOLS	11
CABLE CARS	2
CHAIR LIFTS	30
T-BARS	119
CROSS-COUNTRY SKI RUNS	182 Km
INDOOR SWIMMING POOLS	34
TENNIS HALLS	4
RIDING HALLS	1
SKI KINDERGARTENS	9
HIGHEST MOUNTAIN STATION	2,335 m

LUNGAU 38

The southernmost area of Salzburg Province is gaining in importance among winter holiday makers. Skiing in the south of Radstädter Tauern, in the area of Katschberg, on the inter-valley lift connexion Mauterndorf-St. Michael, St. Margareten-Katschberg and in the mountains called Nockberge. An offer which is really quite impressive. And for a little variation, it's off on a cross-country run or a hike on skis – 124 miles long – through the whole area known as Lungau or on the prepared and cleared hiking paths through a truly magical winter landscape.

Fremdenverkehrsverband Lungau, A-5580 Tamsweg, Rathaus. Tel. 6474/6284, Telex 67798

A-5571 Mariapfarr	6473/278	1.120 m
A-5570 Mauterndorf	6472/7279	1.122 m
A-5562 Obertauern/Tweng	6456/252	1.740 m
A-5582 St. Margarethen	6476/290	1.064 m
A-5582 St. Michael	6477/342	1.075 m
A-5580 Tamsweg	6474/416	1.024 m
A-5591 Thomatal-Schönfeld	6476/250	1.050 m

SKI SCHOOLS	5
CABLE CARS	1
CHAIR LIFTS	7
T-BARS	64
CROSS-COUNTRY SKI RUNS	247 Km
INDOOR SWIMMING POOLS	20
TENNIS HALLS	1
SKI KINDERGARTENS	2
HIGHEST MOUNTAIN STATION	2,360 m

NATIONAL PARK REGION – GOLDBERGE-MÖLLTAL 39

The Grossglockner, the highest and most beautiful mountain in Austria, is on the horizon when you make your ski holidays in Heiligenblut. All the sports in the area, in fact, are undertaken against a backdrop of alpine mountains. First class hotels are harmoniously integrated into the rustic environment. A true marriage of tradition and modern comfort.

A-9831 Flattach	4785/205	750 m
A-9843 Großkirchheim i. M.	4825/212	1.024 m
A-9844 Heiligenblut	4824/2002	1.301 m
A-9815 Kolbnitz-Reißeck	4783/246	600 m
A-9813 Lurnfeld/Möllbrücke	4769/2255	554 m
A-9822 Mallnitz	4784/255	1.200 m
A-9821 Obervellach	4782/2211	700 m
A-9833 Rangersdorf	4823/255	861 m
A-9832 Stall	4823/222	812 m
A-9841 Winklern	4822/227	946 m

SKI SCHOOLS	6
CABLE CARS	1
CHAIR-LIFTS	4
T-BARS	36
CROSS-COUNTRY SKI RUNS	162 Km
INDOOR SWIMMING POOLS	4
TENNIS HALLS	1
RIDING HALLS	1
SKI KINDERGARTENS	5
HIGHEST MOUNTAIN STATION	2,650 m

UPPER DRAUTAL 40

The Upper Drautal awaits its guests with comfortable accommodation in hotels, pensions, country inns and farm houses. This area offers what many people seek but few are lucky enough to find; peace and quiet in beautiful countryside and pure, fresh air. The ice layer on the lake Weissensee covers an area of 2 square miles and reaches a thickness in winter of up to 24 inches. Even horse-drawn sleighs are supported by the ice!

A-9771 Berg im Drautal	4712/532	692 m
A-9772 Dellach im Drautal	4714/234	606 m
A-9761 Greifenburg	4712/216	640 m
A-9773 Irschen	4710/377, 477	809 m
A-9753 Klebach-Lind	4768/217	600 m
A-9781 Oberdrauburg	4710/248, 354	620 m
A-9754 Steinfeld	4717/301, 216	634 m
A-9762 Weißensee-Techendorf	4713/2220	930 m

SKI SCHOOLS	2
T-BARS	10
CROSS-COUNTRY SKI RUNS	100 Km
INDOOR SWIMMING POOLS	3
HIGHEST MOUNTAIN STATION	2,200 m

THE CARNIC SKI AREA 41

The heart of the ski area in Gailtal is the Sonnenalpe Nassfeld at an altitude of 4,800 to 7,000 feet above sea level and situated on the Italian border. The Carnic ski area is considered to be one of those most favoured by heavy snowfall in the entire eastern alpine region. Lesachtal, situated between the Carnic Alps and the Lienz Dolomites, is distinguished by having the most sunshine in the entire alpine area.

A-9635 Dellach im Gailtal	4714/301	675 m
A-9620 Hermagor-Nassfeld	4285/2043	612 m
A-9632 Kirchbach im Gailtal	4284/228	642 m
A-9640 Kötschach-Mauthen	4715/268, 213	710 m
A-9653 Lesachtal	4716/243	1.170 m
A-9623 St. Stefan im Gailtal	4283/2120	725 m
A-9622 Weißbriach/Gitschtal	4286/212	817 m

SKI SCHOOLS	3
CHAIR LIFTS	2
T-BARS	25
CROSS-COUNTRY SKI RUNS	250 Km
INDOOR SWIMMING POOLS	2
TENNIS HALLS	1
SKI KINDERGARTENS	1
HIGHEST MOUNTAIN STATION	1,980 m

THE CENTRAL DRAUTAL AREA 42

The winter-sports fan will find an ideal ski area in Goldeck. There are robust ski-lifts, beautiful slopes, a marked lack of crowds, excellent snow conditions and – lots of sun! Cross-country skiing may be enjoyed on prepared runs as well as ice-skating on the frozen lake of Weissensee. An area with an altitude of around 6,400 feet can be reached by car via Zlan thanks to a newly constructed toll highway.

A-9711 Paternion	4245/2888-0	533 m
A-9713 Stockenboi	4761/214	930 m
A-9721 Weißenstein	4245/385	557 m

T-BARS	9
CROSS-COUNTRY SKI RUNS	82 Km
HIGHEST MOUNTAIN STATION	2,100 m

MILLSTÄTTER SEE 43

Winter holidays in the area around Millstätter See, in the very heart of the famous Carinthian skiing region, is a healthy, sporty pleasure for the whole family. Here you will find a winter with variations: romantic walks in deep snow along well prepared paths. Sports and high spirits in the tennis halls and indoor swimming pools, enjoying ice skating and curling on the frozen lakes (Millstätter Lake, Feldsee and Afritz-See), cross-country skiing or a toboggan party on great slopes on Goldeck and Verditz all are possible here. Then there's that special Austrian hospitality in the evening: there are discos and folklore evenings and après-ski entertainment with your ski-teachers while enjoying all the specialities Carinthia has to offer.

A-9805 Baldramsdorf	4762/7114	554 m
A-9544 Feld am See	4246/2273, 2280	743 m
A-9702 Ferndorf	4245/2086	540 m
A-9360 Fresach	4245/2060	718 m
A-9811 Lendorf	4762/2264	540 m
A-9872 Millstatt	4766/2022, 2021	580 m
A-9545 Radenthein-Döbriach	4246/2288-24	700 m
A-9871 Seeboden	4762/81210	580 m
A-9800 Spittal an der Drau	4762/3420	556 m

SKI SCHOOLS	3
CABLE CARS	1
CHAIR LIFTS	5
T-BARS	17
CROSS-COUNTRY SKI RUNS	233 Km
INDOOR SWIMMING POOLS	2
TENNIS HALLS	2
RIDING HALLS	1
SKI KINDERGARTENS	3
HIGHEST MOUNTAIN STATION	2,050 m

BAD KLEINKIRCHHEIM 44

From mountain to swimming pool can also be a marvellous combination in winter. After fun on the slopes, it's off to the Roman Baths, and after a day of cross-country skiing it's time for Alpine Thermal Baths. After a FIS-slope try the sauna and after your toboggan party jump in the swimming pool. Please come soon!

A-9546 Bad Kleinkirchheim	4240/8212	1.076 m

SKI SCHOOLS	2
CABLE CARS	1
CHAIR LIFTS	4
T-BARS	18
CROSS-COUNTRY SKI RUNS	18 Km
INDOOR SWIMMING POOLS	3
TENNIS HALLS	1
SKI KINDERGARTENS	2
HIGHEST MOUNTAIN STATION	1,917 m

LIESERTAL AND MALTATAL 45

Where the Malta flows into the Lieser lies Gmünd, the Tauern town dating back to the Middle Ages. The local mountain is called Stubeck and can be ascended by ski-lift or properly equipped taxi. It's an area with plenty of snow until well into May with skiing on the Katschberg, which connects Carinthia with Salzburg Province.

A-9853 Gmünd	4732/2197	749 m
A-9861 Krems in Kärnten	4732/2772	800 m
A-9854 Malta	4733/220	832 m
A-9863 Rennweg-Katschberg	4734/330, 208	1.140 m
A-9852 Trebesing	4732/2391	750 m

SKI SCHOOLS	1
CHAIR LIFTS	2
T-BARS	22
CROSS-COUNTRY SKI RUNS	43 Km
INDOOR SWIMMING POOLS	10
TENNIS HALLS	1
SKI KINDERGARTENS	3
HIGHEST MOUNTAIN STATION	2,220 m

THE TURRACH REGION, HOCHRINDL, SIMONHÖHE 46

Experts and Sunday skiers meet here on the same ground. There is something here for everybody. Fans of deep snow are on home ground here — on the Turracher Höhe for example. Nevertheless, you will find that the little villages in the area called Nockgebiet have not turned tourism into a routine. Moreover, this whole area is blessed with a fog-free, southern climate and reputation for mildness. Yet another advantage: it's centrally located in the heart of Carinthia.

A-9571 Albeck/Sirnitz-Hochrindl	4279/32101, 240	800 m
A-9565 Ebene Reichenau-Turracher Höhe	4257/8213, 218	1.065 m
A-9560 Feldkirchen	4276/2511, 2176	560 m
A-9555 Glanegg	4277/276	570 m
A-9563 Gnesau	4278/271	963 m
A-9562 Himmelberg	4276/2310	640 m
A-9560 St. Urban am Urbansee	4277/8311	750 m
A-9571 Steuerberg	4279/221	780 m

SKI SCHOOLS	4
CHAIR LIFTS	2
T-BARS	32
CROSS-COUNTRY SKI RUNS	206 Km
INDOOR SWIMMING POOLS	10
TENNIS HALLS	1
SKI KINDERGARTENS	5
HIGHEST MOUNTAIN STATION	2,280 m

THE WINTER SPORTS AREA AROUND VILLACH 47

The lakes of Carinthia have a special charm out of the swimming season when they are in their "winter look". That's one of the attractions of making your holidays on one of the ski-mountains in the vicinity. The mountain Kanzelhöhe is also popular with non-skiers as an excellent place to get a sun tan. The view of the Karawanken Mountains is superb from here. The Old Town of Villach is another attraction with its cultural treasures, while the thermal baths will help relax and condition your muscles after an exhausting day on the slopes.

A-9601 Arnoldstein	4255/260, 314	564 m
A-9543 Arriach	4247/8514	900 m
A-9530 Bad Bleibergf	4244/211, 280	920 m
A-9583 Faaker See-Finkenstein	4254/2110	560 m
A-9613 Hohenthurn	4256/2267	600 m
A-9611 Nötsch im Gailtal	4256/2145	550 m
A-9570 Ossiach	4243/246	503 m
A-9184 St. Jakob	4253/295, 296	529 m
A-9552 Steindorf	4243/216	510 m
A-9521 Treffen/Sattendorf	4248/2805, 2855	545 m
A-9500 Villach	4242/27288, 23561	500 m
A-9504 Warmbad-Villach	4242/25501	503 m

SKI SCHOOLS	5
CABLE CARS	1
CHAIR LIFTS	8
T-BARS	29
CROSS-COUNTRY SKI RUNS	249 Km
INDOOR SWIMMING POOLS	2
TENNIS HALLS	2
RIDING HALLS	3
SKI KINDERGARTENS	1
HIGHEST MOUNTAIN STATION	1,900 m

THE REGION AROUND WÖRTHER SEE 48

Well prepared runs are ideal for cross-country skiers, ice skating is possible on numerous forest lakes (the lake Saissersee above Velden has its first inviting ice layer already in early December) and you'll find high-spirited action on the frozen surfaces with hockey games underway and other games on ice-skates. By the way: even the smallest ice-skating lakes are constantly cleaned and conditioned. The ski centres of Carinthia are all nearby this famous lake (20 minutes by car) and as a further inducement, prices are very reasonable if you decide to make your winter holidays in the surroundings of Wörther See. It's fun to join in a game of curling; then there is the gambling casino at Velden of course, and other winter pleasures may include a game of bowling or squash and a visit to the sauna. The whole countryside takes on a fairy tale character and it's ideal for long walks, quiet and truly relaxing. More than making up for what it lacks of the pulsating life of the summer months!

A-9020 Klagenfurt	4222/537/222	446 m
A-9062 Moosburg	4272/8184	503 m
A-9220 Velden/ Wörther See	4274/2102	450 m

SKI SCHOOLS	1
T-BARS	4
CROSS-COUNTRY SKI RUNS	256 Km
INDOOR SWIMMING POOLS	2
TENNIS HALLS	8
RIDING HALLS	3
SKI KINDERGARTENS	1
HIGHEST MOUNTAIN STATION	600 m

THE ROSENTAL AREA 49

The valley called Rosental – surrounded by the brilliantly coloured, craggy mountain range of the Karawanken in the south and the low, massive crests to the north – is one of the most beautiful valleys in all Carinthia. It's ideal for long walks and hikes through beautiful countryside thanks to the alpine climate and highly reliable weather. Whether our winter guests are skiers, toboggan fans or enthusiasts for cross-country skiing, they will find lots of snow and many sunny days.

A-9181 Feistritz	4228/2035	545 m
A-9170 Ferlach	4227/2600-31	466 m
A-9072 Ludmannsdorf	4228/2220	540 m
A-9170 Zell	4227/7210	951 m

SKI SCHOOLS	3
T-BARS	8
CROSS-COUNTRY SKI RUNS	71 Km
HIGHEST MOUNTAIN STATION	1,100 m

THE VÖLKERMARKT AREA 50

The Petzen Mountains in winter is a true family ski area, known for its reliable snowfall from the beginning of December until the end of April. There is a chair-lift and four T-bar lifts which facilitate reaching just the right slopes for beginners. experts and everybody in between. The highlight is the 5-mile long slope down to the valley with an altitude drop of 4,100 feet. Bleiberg is known for its ski school, its delightful ski kindergarten and the inviting, well-cared for cross-country ski runs in the valley.

A-9150 Bleiburg	4235/2110	479 m
A-9103 Diex	4232/320511	1.152 m
A-9135 Eisenkappel-Vellach	4238/245, 375	558 m
A-9112 Griffen	4233/247	484 m
A-9473 Neuhaus	4356/20313	442 m
A-9133 Sittersdorf	4237/2020	462 m
A-9100 Völkermarkt	4232/2571-0	462 m

CHAIR LIFTS	1
T-BARS	16
CROSS-COUNTRY SKI RUNS	222 Km
SKI KINDERGARTENS	1
INDOOR SWIMMING POOLS	2
HIGHEST MOUNTAIN STATION	1,950 m

THE ST. VEIT AN DER GLAN AREA 51

An ideal holiday area with a wide range of recreation and sports facilities, a mild climate, sunny days and excellent snow conditions plus wonderful slopes and many lifts, deep snow and the atmospheric world of isolated mountain huts and a warming drink of a potent concoction called ''Hunter's Tea''. Above all, hospitality is the keynote here. An excursion to the 850-year old ducal town of St. Veit an der Glan is well worthwhile. For those with a taste for history, there is a wealth of sights to see, many dating back to Celtic and Roman times. Enjoy the true Austrian-style hospitality of tiny inns and taverns. Quiet hotels, nice pensions and holiday flats will make your holiday a comfortable one. St. Veit an der Glan is the very heart of a large recreation area.

A-9363 Metnitz	4267/220	847 m
A-9300 St. Veit an der Glan	4212/3192-0	518 m
A-9360 Weitensfeld Flattnitz	4265/242-0	1.390 m

CHAIR LIFTS	1
T-BARS	6
CROSS-COUNTRY SKI RUNS	70 Km
INDOOR SWIMMING POOLS	1
SKI KINDERGARTENS	1
HIGHEST MOUNTAIN STATION	1,840 m

THE LAVANTTAL AREA 52

From the mountain peak Hohenwart in Lavanttal, all Carinthia seems to lie at your feet. The panorama extends from the Grossglockner to the Styrian Gesäuse Range. The area called Skialm Klippitzthörl is among the most reliable snowfall areas in southern Austria. Wolfsberg is noted for not only excellent skiing conditions but well cared for hiking paths, skeet shooting, discotheques and the delights of relaxed shopping.

A-9462 Bad St. Leonhard	4350/218	721 m
A-9473 Lavamünd	4356/331, 555	344 m
A-9451 Preitenegg	4353/23108	1.078 m
A-9463 Reichenfels	4359/221	809 m
A-9433 St. Andrä/ Lavanttal	4358/762	443 m
A-9470 St. Paul im Lavanttal	4357/2017	400 m
A-9400 Wolfsberg	4352/3331, 3340	430 m

CHAIR LIFT	1
T-BARS	20
CROSS-COUNTRY SKI RUNS	85 Km
INDOOR SWIMMING POOLS	4
TENNIS HALLS	2
RIDING HALLS	1
SKI KINDERGARTENS	3
HIGHEST MOUNTAIN STATION	2,141 m

WESTERN STYRIA 53

The eastern slopes of the mountain range called Koralpe are noted as a skiing area with excellent recreational character. The slopes are well prepared in the midst of a fine landscape and all the delights of skiing can be enjoyed in this winter wonderland. Mountaineers will appreciate the attraction of the peaks.

A-8524 Bad Gams	3463/2494, 2306	406 m
A-8583 Modriach	3146/2105	1.009 m
A-8583 Pack	3146/8144	1.125 m
A-8592 Salla	3147/206	865 m
A-8553 St. Oswald ob Eibiswald	3468/234, 239	1.050 m
A-8541 Schwanberg	3467/484, 288	418 m
A-8554 Soboth	3460/206	1.065 m
A-8530 Trahütten	3461/231	960 m

SKI SCHOOLS	2
T-BARS	28
CROSS-COUNTRY SKI RUNS	83 Km
INDOOR SWIMMING POOLS	1
TENNIS HALLS	5
SKI KINDERGARTENS	1
HIGHEST MOUNTAIN STATION	1,762 m

MÜRZ VALLEY, BIRTHPLACE OF ROSEGGER, THE STYRIAN SEMMERING, UPPER MÜRZ VALLEY, UPPER FEISTRITZ VALLEY 58

This area is especially popular with Austrians. It lies between the Semmering Pass (Vienna's local skiing area) and the Mürz Valley and is excellent for family-oriented holidays. A dazzling ride by lift brings you to the mountain stations with their magnicent panoramas.

Fremdenverkehrsverband ,,Mürztal''
Raiffeisen-Reisebüro Mürzzuschlag
Hammerpark 5
A-8680 Mürzzuschlag
Tel. 3852/3314, 4330

A-8673 Falkenstein	3173/2410, 2268	1.050 m
A-8654 Fischbach	3170/206, 260	1.050 m
A-8691 Kapellen a.d. Mürz	3857/2281, 2287	702 m
A-8650 Kindberg	3865/2201	555 m
A-8670 Krieglach/Alpl	3855/2404, 2955	608 m
A-8665 Langenwang	3854/2301	637 m
A-8693 Mürzsteg	3859/221	783 m
A-8680 Mürzzuschlag	3852/2460	680 m
A-8692 Neuberg a. d. Mürz	3857/8321	730 m
A-8673 Ratten	3173/2213	765 m
A-8672 Rettenegg	3173/8210, 8252	857 m
A-8672 St. Kathrein am Hauenstein	3173/2271, 2264	822 m
A-8684 Spital/Steinhaus am Semmering	3853/323	800 m

SKI SCHOOLS	5
CHAIR LIFTS	3
T-BARS	60
CROSS-COUNTRY SKI RUNS	200 Km
INDOOR SWIMMING POOLS	4
TENNIS HALLS	2
RIDING HALLS	1
SKI KINDERGARTENS	2
HIGHEST MOUNTAIN STATION	1,350 m

THE HOCHSCHWAB ALPINE AREA 59

The Styrian holiday villages round the Hochschwab are quiet, recreational and offer excellent value. All facilities for skiing include lifts and well cared-for slopes, with plenty of cross-country ski runs as well. In Mariazell, the visitor will get to know Austria's largest pilgrimage church with its basilica and treasury full of magnificent works of art.

Fremdenverkehrsverband ,,Alpenregion Hochschwab-Steiermark'' Stadtamt A-8630 Mariazell Tel. 3882/2244-12

A-8623 Aflenz-Kurort	3861/2265	770 m
A-8614 Breitenau bei Mixnitz	3866/2222	600 m
A-8622 Etmißl	3861/2503	712 m
A-8632 Gußwerk	3882/3246	700 m
A-8630 Halltal	3882/2203	800 m
A-8630 Mariazell	3882/2366	870 m
A-8630 St. Sebastian	3882/2148	820 m
A-8636 Seewiesen	3863/225115	974 m
A-8612 Tragöß	3868/340, 270, 227	780 m
A-8625 Turnau	3863/2234	784 m

SKI SCHOOLS	3
CABLE CARS	1
CHAIR LIFTS	4
T-BARS	42
CROSS-COUNTRY SKI RUNS	106 Km
INDOOR SWIMMING POOLS	3
HIGHEST MOUNTAIN STATION	1,810 m

THE GESÄUSE ALPINE REGION 61

At the foot of this mountain range lies Admont with its famous abbey. The entire region is noted for its fog-free climate and its ski slopes are totally free of avalanche risk. The ski school at St. Gallen also offers courses for senior citizens. A special attraction is winter excursions by horse.

Fremdenverkehrsverband ,,Alpenregion Gesäuse'' Rathaus A-8911 Admont Tel. 3613/2164

A-8911 Admont	3613/2164	641 m
A-8934 Altenmarkt/ St. Gallen	3632/307, 306	461 m
A-8904 Ardning	3616/8201	668 m
A-8920 Hieflau	3634/210	495 m
A-8912 Johnsbach	3611/217	740 m
A-8933 St. Gallen	3632/224, 314	513 m
A-8911 Weng bei Admont	3613/2394	630 m

SKI SCHOOLS	1
T-BARS	18
CROSS-COUNTRY SKI RUNS	122 Km
INDOOR SWIMMING POOLS	1
HIGHEST MOUNTAIN STATION	1,504 m

THE LIESINGTAL ALPINE REGION 62

This area is situated in the heart of Styria and boasts magnificent mountain panoramas. Many peaks are over 6,400 feet high. An internationally known game reserve is located in Mautern. Numerous sports and leisure time facilities are at the disposal of the visitor.

Fremdenverkehrsverband ,,Liesingtal'' A-8774 Mautern Tel. 3845/211, 255

A-8793 Gai	3847/2274	612 m
A-8775 Kalwang	3846/226	753 m
A-8773 Kammern	3844/203	665 m
A-8774 Mautern	3845/211, 255	713 m
A-8772 Traboch	3833/279	629 m
A-8781 Wald am Schoberpaß	3834/250	850 m

SKI SCHOOLS	5
CHAIR LIFTS	1
T-BARS	7
CROSS-COUNTRY SKI RUNS	37 Km
HIGHEST MOUNTAIN STATION	1,150 m

UPPER MURTAL 63

Here you'll find a striking contrast between lively ski atmosphere and quiet, peaceful holiday villages. The ski areas and sports facilities are just as wide ranging. This marvellous mountain landscape is easy to reach and is also ideal for holiday makers with a taste for long walks and hikes in a snowy winter world.

A-8750 Judenburg	3572/3141, 2297	745 m
A-8854 Krakaudorf	3535/282	1.170 m
A-8850 Murau	3532/2720	829 m
A-8742 Obdach/ St. Wolfgang am Zirbitz	3578/203	874 m
A-8832 Oberwölz	3581/420	812 m
A-8762 Oberzeiring	3571/387	932 m
A-8863 Predlitz-Turrach	3534/262	925 m
A-8861 St. Georgen-St. Lorenzen	3537/360	850 m
A-8765 St. Johann am Tauern	3575/217	1.057 m
A-8813 St. Lambrecht	3585/2345	1.072 m

SKI SCHOOLS	7
CHAIR LIFTS	3
T-BARS	46
CROSS-COUNTRY SKI RUNS	256 Km
INDOOR SWIMMING POOLS	4
TENNIS HALLS	1
SKI KINDERGARTENS	2
HIGHEST MOUNTAIN STATION	2,240 m

HEIMAT AM GRIMMING 64

''Heimat am Grimming'' is a true alpine region offering ski facilities on the Planneralm and Riesneralm and the forest area Wörschachwald. Here you will find everything necessary for a relaxing, restful holiday during the winter months. You can experience nature first hand along the cross-country ski runs as well as the numerous hiking paths. Local animals and game can be observed at close quarters at the game reserve in Donnersbachwald.

Fremdenverkehrsverband ,,Heimat am Grimming'' Hauptplatz 49 A-8952 Irdning Tel. 3682/2494

A-8943 Aigen am Putterersee	3682/3540	652 m
A-8953 Donnersbach-Planneralm	3683/234	713 m
A-8953 Donnersbach-wald-Riesneralm	3680/201	960 m
A-8952 Irdning	3682/3243	673 m
A-8903 Liezen-Lassing	3612/8297, 8218	659 m
A-8951 Pürgg-Trauten-fels/Wörschachwald	3682/2911	790 m
A-8954 St. Martin am Grimming	3684/204	716 m
A-8940 Weißenbach bei Liezen	3612/2452, 2207 (22207)	654 m

SKI SCHOOLS	4
CHAIR LIFTS	1
T-BARS	16
CROSS-COUNTRY SKI RUNS	120 Km
INDOOR SWIMMING POOLS	1
TENNIS HALLS	1
RIDING HALLS	1
SKI KINDERGARTENS	1
HIGHEST MOUNTAIN STATION	1,600 m

THE DACHSTEIN-TAUERN AREA 65

The fastest ski slope in the world is one of the ''sport landmarks'' of Schladming. But there is first class skiing on the other slopes as well, plenty of deep snow and beginner's slopes too. There is a wide range of hotel accommodation extending from international first class hotels to modest pensions. For the cross-country skier, there is the unique experience of skiing across the glacier area of Dachstein, which is also noted as a year-round skiing area.

Fremdenverkehrsverband ,,Dachstein-Tauern-Region'' Coburgstraße 52 A-8970 Schladming Tel. 3687/23310

A-8966 Aich-Assach	3686/4305, 4212	694 m
A-8966 Gössenberg	3686/4305, 4616	950 m
A-8962 Gröbming	3685/2131	770 m
A-8967 Haus im Ennstal	3686/2234	740 m
A-8962 Mitterberg	3685/2319	810 m
A-8960 Öblarn	3684/470	668 m
A-8973 Pichl/Mandling	6454/342, 380	799 m
A-8965 Pruggern	3685/2204	681 m
A-8972 Ramsau am Dachstein	3687/81925, 81833	1.100 m
A-8970 Rohrmoose-Untertal	3687/61147	900 m
A-8970 Schladming	3687/22268	749 m

SKI SCHOOLS	11
CABLE CARS	5
CHAIR LIFTS	11
T-BARS	85
CROSS-COUNTRY SKI RUNS	250 Km
INDOOR SWIMMING POOLS	15
TENNIS HALLS	2
SKI KINDERGARTENS	4
HIGHEST MOUNTAIN STATION	2,700 m

THE STYRIAN SALZKAMMERGUT 66

Here you can improve your health and fitness training in more ways than just on the ski slopes. There are cure regimes for liver and gall ailments, as well as treatments for circulatory problems and the respiratory tract. There are plenty of delightful meeting places for relaxation after skiing or after daily treatments. The winter holidaymaker will also learn about ancient traditions and customs which are kept alive in the villages and towns round the lakes.

Fremdenverkehrsverband ,,Steirisches Salzkammergut'' Kurkommission Bad Aussee
A-8990 Bad Aussee
Tel. 6152/2323

A-8992 Altaussee	6152/71643	723 m
A-8990 Bad Aussee	6152/2323	659 m
A-8983 Bad Mitterndorf	6153/2444	809 m
A-8993 Grundlsee	6152/8666	732 m
A-8984 Pichl/Kainisch	6154/201	810 m
A-8982 Tauplitz/ Tauplitzalm	3688/466, 304	896 m

SKI SCHOOLS	**7**
CHAIR LIFTS	**3**
T-BARS	**38**
CROSS-COUNTRY SKI RUNS	**95 Km**
INDOOR SWIMMING POOLS	**2**
TENNIS HALLS	**2**
RIDING HALLS	**2**
SKI KINDERGARTENS	**5**
HIGHEST MOUNTAIN STATION	**1,965 m**

PYHRN-EISENWURZEN 67

This area is known as a true delight for experts thanks to its authentic alpine character and technically excellent ski facilities. Here, mountaineering enthusiasts, ski fans and even holiday-makers without any fondness for sports all meet on common ground. There is plenty to do, with traditional folklore events and carnival parades adding to attractions.

Ferienregion Pyhrn-Eisenwurzen
A-4560 Kirchdorf, Hauptplatz 20,
Tel. 7852/2450

A3334 Gaflenz- Forsteralm	7446/205	476 m
A-4573 Hinterstoder	7564/5263	600 m
A-4564 Klaus	7585/255	470 m
A-4582 Spital/Pyhrn	7563/249	650 m
A-4452 Ternberg	7256/255	350 m
A-4574 Vorderstoder	7564/8255	808 m
A-4580 Windischgarsten	7562/266	601 m

SKI SCHOOLS	**5**
CABLE CARS	**1**
CHAIR LIFTS	**7**
T-BARS	**42**
CROSS-COUNTRY SKI RUNS	**200 Km**
INDOOR SWIMMING POOLS	**13**
TENNIS HALLS	**7**
RIDING HALLS	**5**
SKI KINDERGARTENS	**2**
HIGHEST MOUNTAIN STATION	**1,867 m**

SALZKAMMERGUT 68

The area known as Salzkammergut is internationally known for its fairy tale atmosphere; a brilliant mosaic of lakes and mountains, especially popular in summer. Thanks to new technical installations, this area is now well equipped for winter sports as well. Truly excellent hotels are an attraction too. The Salzkammergut is particularly well located and easy to reach.

Salzkammergutverband
A-4820 Bad Ischl
Tel. 6132/3520, Telex 68117

A-4813 Altmünster	7612/8611/40	443 m
A-4822 Bad Goisern	6135/8329	500 m
A-4820 Bad Ischl	6132/3520	470 m
A-4802 Ebensee	6133/8016	425 m
A-4810 Gmunden	7612/4305	420 m
A-4824 Gosau	6136/295	750 m
A-4645 Grünau im Almtal	7616/8268	527 m
A-4830 Hallstatt	6134/208	508 m
A-5310 Mondsee	6232/2270	481 m
A-4831 Obertraun	6134/351	514 m
A-5360 St. Wolfgang	6138/2239	540 m
A-4644 Scharnstein	7615/340	501 m
A-4852 Weyregg am Attersee	7664/236	480 m

SKI SCHOOLS	**8**
CABLE CARS	**9**
CHAIR LIFTS	**5**
T-BARS	**58**
CROSS-COUNTRY SKI RUNS	**140 Km**
INDOOR SWIMMING POOLS	**13**
TENNIS HALLS	**6**
RIDING HALLS	**2**
SKI KINDERGARTENS	**3**
HIGHEST MOUNTAIN STATION	**2,075 m**

MÜHLVIERTEL 71

The so-called Mühlviertel describes an area stretching between the Bavarian Forest and the region known as Waldviertel and is characterized by medium altitude mountains. There are large ski areas and cross-country runs of over 460 miles at altitudes between 2,900 and 4,300 feet. Most of the cross-country skiing areas offer sufficient snow from mid-December until the end of March. Cross-country skiing can be enjoyed here at every grade of difficulty, a fact clearly shown by the choice of the Mühlviertel as training site for the Austrian national cross-country skiing team.

Fremdenverkehrsverband Mühlviertel
A-4020 Linz, Starhembergstraße 35a
Tel. 732/52424/25, Telex 22625

A-4190 Bad Leonfelden	7213/397	749 m
A-4240 Freistadt	7942/2974	560 m
A-4170 Haslach	7289/555	531 m
A-4202 Hellmonsödt	7215/348	824 m
A-4163 Klaffer	7288/26615	642 m
A-4251 Sandl	7944/250	927 m
A-4172 St. Johann am Wimberg	7217/26105	720 m
A-4164 Schwarzenberg	7290/27107	786 m
A-4161 Ulrichsberg	7288/255	626 m

CHAIR LIFTS	**1**
T-BARS	**56**
CROSS-COUNTRY SKI RUNS	**780 Km**
INDOOR SWIMMING POOLS	**22**
TENNIS HALLS	**3**
RIDING HALLS	**6**
SKI KINDERGARTENS	**1**
HIGHEST MOUNTAIN STATION	**1,337 m**

ALPINE FOOTHILLS 74

This area has a ski tradition dating back to the beginning of the century: the first slalom race ever held took place here in 1905. Today, a great variety of technically excellent skiing areas may be found here. The slopes of Hochkar and Lackenhof in the Ötscher Mountain Range are noted for reliable snowfall. Each and every mountain is worth visiting for magnificent panoramas and vistas.

Region Voralpenland,
Volksfestplatz 3
A-3250 Wieselburg
Tel. 7416/2191

A-3222 Annaberg	2728/8245	973 m
A-3292 Gaming	7485/308	390 m
A-3345 Göstling an der Ybbs	7484/2204	532 m
A-3343 Hollenstein an der Ybbs	7445/218	487 m
A-3295 Lackenof am Ötscher	7480/286	810 m
A-3180 Lilienfeld	2762/2212	377 m
A-3293 Lunz am See	7486/310	610 m
A-3224 Mitterbach am Erlaufsee	3882/2126	800 m
A-3214 Puchenstuben	2726/238	871 m
A-3193 St. Aegyd am Neuwalde	2768/290	600 m
A-3184 Türnitz	2769/204	463 m
A-3340 Waidhofen an der Ybbs	7442/2511	358 m
A-3341 Ybbsitz	7443/340	404 m

SKI SCHOOLS	**11**
CHAIR LIFTS	**9**
T-BARS	**88**
CROSS-COUNTRY SKI RUNS	**148 Km**
INDOOR SWIMMING POOLS	**11**
TENNIS HALLS	**1**
RIDING HALLS	**1**
SKI KINDERGARTENS	**3**
HIGHEST MOUNTAIN STATION	**1,799 m**

"GEMUTLICHKEIT"

A winter holiday in Austria is more than a great skiing experience. It means a warmth of hospitality, traditional resorts, friendliness of the people, good food, cosy atmospheres, sophisticated nightlife for those who want it or the simple pleasures of a horse-drawn sleigh. Above all, Gemutlichkeit means a feeling that one really belongs. Austria, for the complete winter holiday.

GLOSSARY

Anticipation
Generally preparing yourself for the next action. Is also used to denote the turning of the hips to facilitate the swing.

Banking
Leaning the body into the curve of the swing to counteract the centrifugal forces exerted on it.

Centrifugal Force
The force which pushes the skier to the outside of the curve and which can be counteracted by leaning into it whilst setting the edges of the skis in the snow.

Downhill Ski
Term denoting the ski furthest from the hill in a traverse or swing (may also be called the outside ski). This downhill ski becomes the inside ski of the curve when the swing is initiated and in turn becomes the uphill ski once the fall-line is crossed.

Edge Change
Changing the pressure on the skis from one edge to the other.

Edging
Applying pressure to the edges of the skis.

Fall-Line
An imaginary line which follows the steepest line of descent down the slope.

Initiation
The moment at which the swing is set into motion.

Inside Ski
The term denoting the ski on the inside of the curve during the swing. Also used to denote the uphill ski in a swing or traverse.

Leg Action
Using legs whilst keeping upper body quiet.

Mogul
In skiing, general term for a bump caused by the criss-crossing and turning action of skis.

Momentum
The force produced by the combined weight and movement of the skier.

Outside Ski
The term denoting the ski on the outside of the curve during the swing. Also used to denote the downhill ski in a swing or traverse.

Pedalling
Bending of one leg while straightening the other causing a transfer of weight.

Pressure
Voluntary or involuntary force applied to the skis either by the skier or the terrain.

Schuss
Straight running of the skier down the fall-line.

Scissors
Opening one ski to make a scissors shape, i.e. one ski divergent from the other in the direction of travel.

Side-slip
A sideways movement of the skis down or across the slope, controlled by the degree of edging.

Side Stepping
Stepping uphill on the edges of the skis at right angles to the slope.

Skidding
Voluntary or involuntary pressure on the flat base of the skis causing them to slide sideways.

Snowplough
Placing the two skis at an angle to the direction of travel with the tips converging.

Stem
Placing one ski at an angle to direction of travel with the skis converging at the tips.

Stepping
The action of opening the skis by a step movement as opposed to sliding them apart.

The Swing
Austrian Ski School terminology for all the actions involved in making linked changes in direction.

The Swings
(Stem opening uphill ski)
The uphill ski is placed in a converging position to the downhill ski in order to initiate the swing.

(Stem opening downhill ski)
The downhill ski is placed in a converging position to the uphill ski in order to thrust off to initiate the swing.

(Parallel opening uphill ski)
Stepping out of uphill ski keeping it parallel to downhill ski to initiate the swing.

(Parallel opening downhill ski)
The downhill ski is placed at a narrow angle to the uphill ski in order to allow thrust off to initiate the swing.

(Parallel with up-unweighting)
Straightening the legs to momentarily reduce pressure on the skis which are swung around in parallel to initiate the swing.

(Parallel with down-unweighting)
Allowing the legs to be bent progressively to reduce pressure on the skis in order to initiate the swing.

(Scissors opening uphill ski)
A dynamic placement of the uphill ski in a divergent position to the downhill ski to initiate the swing.

(Scissors opening downhill ski)
Dynamic pressure of the previous swing opens the downhill ski into a divergent position from which the swing is initiated.

Tracking
The ski's ability to maintain line and direction.

Traverse
Moving across the slope on the uphill edges of the skis.

Up-extension
Straightening the legs to adopt a more upright position. May also be used to describe the action of up-unweighting.

Uphill Ski
Term denoting the ski nearest the hill in a traverse or swing (may also be called the inside ski). This uphill ski becomes the outside ski as the swing is initiated and in turn becomes the downhill ski once the fall-line is crossed.

Wedeln
German for 'tail-wag'. Elegant series of short linked swings.

Weighting
Increasing the pressure on one or both skis.

Weight Shift
Dynamic transfer of some or all weight from one ski to the other or from the tips to the tails of the skis or vice-versa.

INDEX

N

Nansen, Fridtjof 9, 10
Norwegian technique 9, 10

P

parallel swing 12, 72
    opening the uphill ski 44,
    47, 54-57
    opening the downhill ski
    44, 47, 58-61
    with the up-
    unweighting 44, 48, 62-63
    with the down-
    unweighting 44, 48, 64-67,
    96
pedalling 58, 66
piste machines 92, 93
piste map 94-95
'practice deep snow' 96, 98
preparation methods 18-19

R

races 12, 13
    children 86-87
    Hahnenkamm Run 118-19
    Kandahar 12, 13
    slalom 12, 84, 113, 114-15
    WISBI 80-81, 82-83, 112,
    113
    WISLI 82, 134
Red Devils 100-01
Reinl, Kurt 11
resorts, map of 138-39
route signs 93

S

Saalbach-Hinterglemm piste
    map 94-95
safety 91-93, 120
    deep snow rules 98-99
    on ski lifts 36-37
Sailer, Toni 85
Schneider, Hannes 10, 11, 12,
    122

schools 80-81
    Arlberg 9, 10, 12
    Federal Ski School, St
    Christoph 14-17
Schranz, Karl 13
schussing 30-31, 39, 96, 133
scissors swing 56
    opening the uphill ski 44,
    49, 70-73
    opening the downhill ski
    44, 49, 74-77
Seefeld 136-37
Seelos, Toni 12
shoes, cross-country 128
side-slipping 35, 39
side-step 32, 134
Siitonen step 127, 134, 135
skating step 72, 77, 134
skidding 30, 31, 40, 42-43,
    50, 72, 102
skis
    carrying 23
    choice 22
    cross-country 128, 134
    deep snow 100
    maintenance 22
    Norwegian 9
    preparation 23
    turning 40-41
slalom gates 39, 50, 52, 56,
    60, 62, 66, 86, 112
slalom racing 12, 84, 113,
    114-15
slalom skiing 112, 13
snowplough 31, 39, 50
stem swing 96
    opening the uphill ski 44,
    46, 50-51, 102
    opening the downhill ski
    44, 46, 52-53, 102
steps
    cross-country 134-35
    diagonal 130-31
    herringbone 32, 134
    side-step 32, 134
    Siitonen 127, 134, 135
    skating 72, 77, 134
step swing 117
sticks, cross-country 128
straight running 30-31, 39,
    133
swing 39, 40-41, 44-45, 86,
    96, 100, 104, 117, 120,
    122

carved 42-43
garland 35, 39
moguls 102, 104
parallel 12, 44, 47-48, 54-
67, 72, 96
scissors 44, 49, 56, 70-77
stem 44, 46, 50-53, 96,
102
step 117
to the hill 38-39
wedeln 12, 13, 39, 68-69,
96
see also turns

T

teachers see instructors
traversing 30, 34-35, 39, 96
tuck position 108, 118, 119
turns 10, 11, 12, 28, 30, 32,
    84
    carving 30, 40, 42-43, 72
    how skis turn 40-41
    kick 32
    waltz 122
    see also swing

V

von Lerch, Major Theodor 9

W

walking 32
    diagonal step 130-31
    herringbone 32
    level ground 32
    side-step 32
Wallner, Josef 9
waltz turn 122
warming up 28-29
wedeln 12, 13, 39, 68-69, 96
wind resistance 118
WISBI races 80-81, 82-83,
    112, 113
WISLI races 82, 134

Z

Zdarsky, Matthias 8, 9, 10, 12,
    122

ACKNOWLEDGEMENTS

James Wotton and Graham Davis wish to thank the following for their valuable contributions to the preparation of this book

For translating the original manuscript Tek Translations Ltd

SUB EDITING
Sam Elder

DESIGNERS
Kevin Ryan
Sarah Collins
Sara Woolcombe
Lucy Adams
Gill Sermon

ILLUSTRATION AND ARTWORK
David Lawrence
Hussein Hussein
The Smith Brown
Partnership

PHOTOGRAPHER
Kjell Langset

PHOTOGRAPHS
Professor Hoppichler
Bertle Auer
Toni Hofer
Mark Junak – Bladon Lines
The Tourist Offices of
St. Anton
Lech
Ischgl
Kitzbühel
Igls
Niederau
Soll
Saalbach-Hinterglemm
Zell am See
Schladming
Seefeld